The Healthy Small Church

The Healthy Small Church

Diagnosis and Treatment for the Big Issues

Dennis Bickers

BEACON HILL PRESS
OF KANSAS CITY

Copyright 2005
by Dennis Bickers and Beacon Hill Press of Kansas City

ISBN 978-0-8341-2240-6

Printed in the
United States of America

Cover Design: J. R. Caines

All Scripture quotations are from the *New King James Version* (NKJV). Copyright ©
1979, 1980, 1982 Thomas Nelson, Inc.

Library of Congress Cataloging-in-Publication Data

Bickers, Dennis W., 1948-
    The healthy small church : diagnosis and treatment for the big issues / Dennis Bickers.
        p. cm.
    Includes bibliographical references.
    ISBN 0-8341-2240-5 (pbk.)
    1. Small churches. 2. Pastoral theology. I. Title.

    BV637.8.B53 2006
    254—dc22

                                                                    2005031736

10 9 8 7 6 5 4

Contents

Acknowledgments and Dedication

Once again it has been a joy to work with Beacon Hill Press in bringing these thoughts to the printed page. I appreciate their belief in the importance of this project and in the value of small churches. Richard Buckner, thank you for believing in this book and for your encouragement. Your thoughtful editing and recommendations have made this a much better book. Jonathan Wright has also been a great encourager and challenged me to clarify some of my thoughts, making this a much better resource for small-church leaders. On behalf of the readers, thank you, Richard and Jonathan.

One of our great joys in our lives is our grandchildren. Their laughter, their sense of wonder, and even their endless questions bring great delight to Faye and me. Yet I often wonder about the world they're entering. They face challenges and difficulties that I never faced at their age. They'll need a light to help them through their life's journeys, and that light will come through their relationships with the Lord Jesus Christ and their churches. I deeply want our churches to be healthy, because our children and grandchildren need healthy churches to successfully navigate through life.

Tyler, Alex, Rebekah, Colin, and Grace, my prayer for you every day is that you'll grow up to be godly men and women, leaders in your homes, churches, and communities. Every day your granny and I pray for your safety and well-being, and we pray that you'll continually grow closer to God. This book is dedicated to you.

Introduction

For 20 years I served as a bivocational pastor for a small rural church in Indiana. I resigned from that congregation to accept a position as an area minister with the American Baptist Churches of Indiana and Kentucky. In this new ministry I work with 80 churches in my area. Half of these churches average 50 people or fewer on Sunday mornings. Since the release of my first book, *The Tentmaking Pastor*, I've had the opportunity to work with several small churches, their pastors, and denominational leaders from various states. Along the way I've learned some things about small churches:

- Many suffer from serious self-esteem issues. They can't see themselves as churches God can significantly use. They often tell me that their task is to be a place where student pastors can learn how to be ministers so they'll be prepared when they leave for their next pastorate. I usually ask them to show me where the Bible says that's the mission for any church.
- Most of them lack any common vision except for survival. This often causes the church to plateau and eventually decline.
- Some are very exclusive due to the strong family ties that exist within the church. This can make it very difficult for new people to feel welcome, and it limits the growth of the church. It can also mean that even the pastor will find it difficult to be accepted and unable to exercise any real leadership.
- Resources are usually limited. Enough money comes in to pay the bills and other essentials, but there may not be enough to fund new programs or ministries. Interestingly enough, if an emergency arises within the church, the money always turns up to meet that emergency.
- Too much is frequently expected of the pastor. I have talked with many pastors who are expected to mow the grass, change the light bulbs, drive the bus, paint the parsonage, and prepare two sermons and a Bible study each week. Visitation and evangelism are also the pastor's job. After all, that's why the church pays him $15,000 a year.
- Leadership is in the hands of a few people who may or may not be spiritually qualified to exercise such leadership. Sometimes these leadership positions are protected by serious turf wars.

These unhealthful qualities exist in many small churches and are often the reason the church has failed to grow. The good news is that each of these can be overcome, and an unhealthy church can become a healthy church capable of experiencing growth. This book addresses the qualities of a healthy small church and shares some ways to achieve those qualities.

Please don't think I've met only unhealthy small churches. I've seen many healthy ones and have observed several things about them:

- They have a very positive self-image. They don't equate church size with church significance. They understand that God has placed them in their community to represent Him as they minister to the needs of the community.
- The church shares a common vision that gives it a sense of purpose and unity. Rather than being pulled in many different directions, it's moving forward to accomplish its God-given task.
- Although family ties and community are important, those who visit the church are warmly welcomed and affirmed. These guests often return and may later join the church, simply because of the way they were treated.
- Church members understand the importance of faithful stewardship and financially support the ministry of the church. Such a church routinely receives more than its budget requirements each week, which allows it to develop new ministries and programs. This also enables the congregation to support mission work around the world. Such a church may give 10 to 20 percent of its weekly offerings to its denominational mission work.
- Ministry is understood to be the responsibility of all the members of the church, not just the pastor. Laypeople are involved in outreach and visitation programs. They often lead the worship service, and sometimes they fill the pulpit when the pastor is away. Members seek opportunities to learn more so they can be better equipped to serve.
- People are encouraged to serve according to their spiritual gifts, not by their seniority in the church. Leadership positions are filled by those who have gifts in leadership and who are spiritually qualified.

Some of these healthy churches were once unhealthy churches that may not have exhibited any of these positive qualities. Their ability to transform themselves should serve as an inspiration to every church that may be struggling with unhealthful symptoms. Transformation is never easy, but it's always worth it. It's also not accomplished very quickly. I often tell people that anything worthwhile that happens in a church usually takes much longer than you would have hoped.

Church health is never permanent. Just as people need regular checkups to ensure a healthier life, churches should regularly check themselves for symptoms that would indicate that something might be wrong. This book can be used as a diagnostic tool for a small church that wants to get healthy and remain that way.

The first chapter explores the importance of the small church. Despite what some critics might say, the small church does offer some important benefits to its members and to society. Chapter 2 helps define church health. It always helps to be able to identify our goal. The remaining chapters explore various qualities of church health, especially as they relate to the smaller church. These chapters can give you the tools to examine your church for signs of health.

If you're the pastor of a small church, I would suggest that first you get familiar with this book. Then involve some of your church leaders to study it with you, and involve them in the diagnosis of your church.

The final chapter includes a number of diagnostic questions that you and your church leadership can use to determine the health of your church. Most likely, the church will score well in some qualities and not so well in others. You'll need the assistance of the church leaders to help turn around the areas of weakness that are identified. Their assistance will be easier to obtain if they've been involved in the diagnostic stage with you.

The Importance of Small Churches

Healthy small churches provide people with the opportunity to enjoy community and be involved in ministry in a family-type atmosphere.

—Dennis Bickers

Abraham Lincoln said, "The Lord prefers common-looking people. That's the reason he made so many of them." The same might be said of small churches. Although much is written about megachurches, we're simply a nation of small churches. Approximately two-thirds of all churches in the United States average 100 people or fewer on Sundays. More than 100,000 churches average 50 people or fewer in their Sunday morning attendance.

Small churches can be found in every denomination and among every ethnic group. Some of these are new church plants, while others have been around for 150 years or longer. They are found in the rural countryside, small towns, and large urban areas. Some were once large churches until population shifts, church splits, or something else occurred to cause them to lose their large membership. Others started small and remained that way due to many different factors.

Several years ago denominations began to encourage their churches to grow larger. Resources and programs were developed for the larger churches and for those who wanted to grow larger. Smaller churches were sometimes closed or merged with other churches. Fewer and fewer resources were developed specifically for the smaller church. Some denominations began to require a seminary education prior to a minister being ordained, and smaller churches often found they could not afford a seminary-trained pastor.

In more recent years we've seen great interest in the megachurches, such as Willow Creek Community Church, near Chicago, and Saddleback Church, near Los Angeles. Pastors and church leaders flock to leadership conferences hosted by these and other large churches, hoping to find a program or an idea that will help them grow their church into a megachurch. Often these leaders experience more disappointment than growth when they return to their churches.

There's nothing wrong with large churches, of course, but there's also nothing wrong with small churches. Some small churches will never experience great numerical growth, but that doesn't mean they're not important or that they have little to contribute. Small churches contribute much to their membership and communities.

People Experience Community in Small Churches

I sometimes tell congregations that we should pattern our churches after the theme song from the television program *Cheers*, which spoke of a place where everybody knew your name. Although churches are far removed from bars, people everywhere are looking for that kind of relationship with others. People want to be known, accepted, and loved for who they are. They can often find this acceptance in the smaller church.

Larger churches often promote small groups within the church so their members can have more intimate relationships with others. The small church is already a small group where such relationships can develop. When a person becomes a member of a small congregation, he or she doesn't just join a church—he or she becomes a member of the family.

This community is experienced in many ways. In my pastoral ministry we had a time in the worship service in which people could share their stories of praise and any prayer concerns they might have. In larger churches there isn't time for this type of sharing, but in the small church this is important. Not only did we know about the good things that were happening within our church family, but we also knew some concerns that our congregation was feeling.

Community is experienced in the board meetings and business meetings of the small church. Early in my ministry our board meetings frustrated me. The meeting might last for two hours with no more than 30 minutes of actual business discussed. During the meeting we would talk about how the crops were doing, swap fishing and hunting stories, and reminisce about people and things that happened in the church 40 years earlier. I sometimes wondered if we would ever get around to discussing church issues. I later came to understand that small churches are centered on relationships, and these discussions simply came from the relationships these people had with one another. In many cases they were as important as the church items we needed to discuss.

Community is also seen as people talk with one another before and after the worship service. It's a sign of church health when people are in no hurry to leave the church building at the close of the worship service. In a healthy relationship people enjoy being with one another and talking about their lives. A small church offers them the opportunity to do that. The importance of community and how the small church can meet this need are covered in more detail in chapter 9.

People Have an Opportunity to Serve and Use Their Gifts

A large church once called in a consultant to help find out why so few people were joining the church. The consultant asked the pastor how long it would be between when a person joined the church and the time he or she was able to serve in the church in some significant capacity. After considering the question for some time, the pastor answered that it would probably be about 10 years! The consultant identified that as one reason the church was not seeing many people become members.

Studies have proven that people want to join a church in which they can become involved. For two years Thom Ranier conducted a study on formerly unchurched people who joined a church. One of the findings that came out of that study was as follows:

> The formerly unchurched deeply desire to be a part of a church that makes a difference. They want to be involved in small groups, Sunday school, and ministry. They want to participate in a church that has clear direction and vision. And they do not mind, indeed they desire, churches that expect them to do ministry for God in the church where they met Christ.[1]

Small churches give everybody the opportunity to serve in the various ministries of the church. In fact, these churches have to be careful that they don't overburden new members with too many responsibilities. I know of one church that tried to talk a new Christian into teaching a Sunday School class within a few weeks of joining the church. Fortunately, the individual understood that he was not prepared to teach a class. However, there were other opportunities for this person to serve within the church, and he has been a very active member of his congregation.

Small Churches Communicate Quickly When Problems Arise

Never underestimate the power of the church grapevine. While it obviously can be used in negative ways when people are disgruntled, it can also enable a church to respond very quickly when a member is in need. Many small churches establish prayer chains so that members can pray for one another when needs arise. The church family can be contacted in a very short time with such prayer chains. Needs other than prayer can also be determined at this time and shared with one another. From personal experience I can assure you that it's comforting to know that the entire church family is praying for you when you're going through a difficult challenge.

I recently met with the pastor and members of a small church to discuss some changes they want to make in their church. When I asked them to identify some of the strengths of the church, the first one mentioned was their prayer chain. One lady mentioned that not only were prayer concerns shared with one another, but other issues important to the church and community were also quickly relayed to members of the congregation.

People Share Common Experiences

Members of the small church often share very similar life experiences. Work experience, economic status, education level, racial and cultural background, language, and age may be very similar among members of the small church. It's also not uncommon for many in the smaller church to be connected through marriage. I know some small churches where 50 to 75 percent of the members are related through blood or marriage. This certainly has an impact on the sense of community in the church, and it also may have an impact on the church calendar. Church events are often scheduled around family reunions or other gatherings of the larger families of the congregation.

A small rural church knows that the spring and fall months are not a good time to schedule revival services or other major emphases in the church if many of its members are involved in agriculture. These members will focus on getting their crops into the ground or harvesting the crops during these months. Such churches also know not to schedule anything special during the first few days of hunting season if they want the men involved in the activity.

People Are More Important than Programs or Performances

As stated previously, small-church pastors will often experience great frustration when they return from church growth conferences. While at the conference they may have heard about a program they believe would work very well in their churches. When they return to their churches, however, they find the people much less excited about that program than they are. Typically a church will ask questions about how the program will affect them, the current members. If they perceive that it might affect the sense of community in the church, they're likely to reject it.

Small churches are also more interested in community than in performance. One good example is found in the worship services. Laypeople in these churches often lead congregational singing. Sometimes a layperson cannot read music and may not even be able to carry a tune, but that often doesn't matter to the small church. What does matter is that this person has led the music in that church for 20 years. What matters even more is that when the church kitchen had a fire a few years earlier, he was there every Saturday helping the men rebuild the kitchen, and his family replaced the refrigerator.

Community Benefits

The community surrounding the small church benefits from the presence of the church. In many places the small church still serves as a meeting place for the community. It may serve as a building where people vote in local and national elections. Community youth groups such as scouts or 4-H may use the church building as their meeting place. People in the community often want to be married in the small neighborhood church.

Small churches serve their communities by providing assistance to people in trouble. The church I served helped many people pay rent and utility bills and bought food for people who requested our help. Because of limited resources, we could not help everyone who approached us, but many larger churches have the same limitations.

A few years ago a nearby river overflowed its banks and caused great damage. One small community was particularly hit hard, resulting in many people being homeless and without basic services. A small church in that community immediately became the assistance center. That church's denomination sent disaster relief money to the church. Other area churches provided money and volunteer help.

Meals were prepared and served to the residents of that community. Other basic needs were met, and when the river went down, the volunteers helped with the cleanup. That small church doesn't average more than 30 people on Sunday mornings, but it served its community well in a time of great need.

The small church also provides its community with a sense of hope and an awareness of God. Some people may live almost within the shadow of the steeple but never attend the church services. However, the mere presence of the church gives them a sense of strength and hope. The small church makes a powerful statement every time a person passes it. When life begins to crumble around these people, they're often attracted to that small church in their community to see if there are any answers to be found there that can help them. In a healthy small church they'll find those answers and will often find a personal relationship with Jesus Christ.

I believe God still uses small churches in big ways. They're important to the kingdom of God because of the impact they can have on the people surrounding them. The challenge is to find ways to help these churches become and remain healthy so they can fulfill the task God has given them. The following chapters will help us find those ways.

2
The Problem of Unhealthy Churches

I believe the key issue for churches in the twenty-first century will be church health, not church growth.[1]

—Rick Warren

It was time for my physical examination. For two hours I entered various rooms in the medical complex to donate fluids; have my hearing and vision checked; be X-rayed, poked, prodded; and experience my first stress test. A week later I returned to the office to hear the report. After reviewing the documents, the doctor announced, "You're in pretty good shape for a man your age." Although the last part of that statement made me wince, I was glad to hear that I was in good general health. The doctor was especially pleased that medication had lowered my elevated blood pressure to acceptable levels.

The high blood pressure had been discovered two years earlier during a similar physical exam. At that time I began to learn as much about it as I could. Hypertension is sometimes known as the "silent killer," because, if left unchecked, it can affect the heart, kidneys, and arteries and can lead to atherosclerosis or stroke. There may be no symptoms to warn the individual that anything is wrong until the damage has been done. With a family history that includes strokes and heart problems, I knew it was important to get this disease under control. Along with the medication, I try to watch my diet and exercise more, and my blood pressure has been under control for several years now.

Like our bodies, a church can have a relatively minor problem that, if left unchecked, can begin to affect the entire system. There might not be any symptoms for a number of years, but unresolved problems will eventually cause serious issues and can lead to the death of the church.

What are some of the problems that can lead to a church's becoming unhealthy?

- **Conflict.** Conflict cannot be avoided in a church and doesn't actually have to be unhealthful. We'll see in a later chapter that there are several ways to handle conflict. However, unresolved conflict in a congregation will always resurface and prevent the church from moving forward.
- **Focusing inward.** Churches in trouble tend to become more focused on their issues rather than focusing on the needs around them. Unhealthy churches focus most of their attention on satisfying their members' needs, while healthy churches focus on transforming people's lives and society.[2] A church that's focused on itself and its survival is in serious trouble.
- **Cultural indifference.** Too many congregations are fond of living in the 1950s. They can't understand the culture in which we live today, nor do they really want to. They continue to offer a flannelgraph ministry to people with iPods, PalmPilots, and computers and wonder why they're not interested. Incidentally, my computer's spell-checker indicates that "flannelgraph" is not even a recognized word. That should tell us something!
- **Poor leadership.** This will also be addressed at length in a later chapter, but poor leadership, both pastoral and lay, severely limits a church's effectiveness.
- **Lack of vision and purpose.** Too many small churches are content to survive. Anything that appears to threaten that survival is immediately rejected, although that might be the very thing that would restore vitality to the church.
- **Poor self-esteem.** It's believed by some that "raising the esteem of small congregations will top the church's agenda for the next few decades."[3]

These are just a few of the many issues that create an unhealthy church environment. An unhealthy church can't produce good ministry. Jesus tells us, "A good tree cannot bear bad fruit, nor can a bad tree bear good fruit" (Matt. 7:18).

George Barna describes many of these churches when he writes,

Thousands of churches across America have deteriorated to the point where they are a ministry in theory only, a shell of what they had once been. In these churches, little if any outreach or inreach takes place. The name and buildings may insinuate a church is present, but lives are not touched in a significant, spiritual way by such artifacts. As long as these churches have a handful of faithful attenders and can afford some meeting space and a speaker, they remain in existence. They have, however, essentially completed their life as a church.[4]

As painful as these comments are to read, there's little doubt that they're true. All across our continent and in every denomination, scores of small churches struggle to exist. Certainly none of these churches intended for this to happen. At one time many of them were vibrant, exciting places of ministry, but that was long ago. Unhealthful habits and attitudes have robbed these churches of their vitality.

"Many congregations today have been in decline for years but are unwilling to face that hard truth. These churches are fond of saying, 'This is a great place. We really love one another.' But they are not willing to admit that they are dying a slow death that is robbing the next generation of an opportunity to know the gospel."[5]

Obtain Assistance with the Diagnostic Process

The first step an addict must take toward recovery is to admit that he or she has a problem and needs help. If we find ourselves in an unhealthy church, the first step we need to take is to admit that this is the case and seek ways to restore health. However, this first step may be the most difficult. It's painful for a struggling church to look at itself. Most churches would do well to have someone outside of their body come in and help with this process.

A denominational church can invite someone from their headquarters, district, or conference to help them identify issues they need to address. Periodically, one of the 80 churches I serve will ask me to meet with the leadership, or even the entire congregation at times, to address issues and help them determine direction. I recently met with a congregation that has space limitations affecting its ability to grow. We discussed some practical aspects of building new facilities, but we also discussed outreach strategies and vision. At the end of the evening the church had some new questions to answer, but that process will help them prepare for a more effective ministry in the future.

Many denominational organizations are becoming more proactive in helping churches address issues that can help them become healthier. Our region's churches recently completed a four-year event called "Church Alive," in which we worked with a number of churches in our region on issues of church transformation. The materials and speakers we brought in were excellent. Participating churches met in cluster

groups to learn from one another and to explore the topics we introduced in greater detail. Many of these churches continued on to transformation in exciting ways.

We completed "Church Alive" and replaced it with a new process
we call "Church Alive Next Generation," which we offer to churches
one-on-one rather than in a cluster format, and we tailor it to the specific needs of each congregation that wants to work with us. We believe this will lead to healthier churches that will be better able to fulfill the task God has given them. Currently four churches in my area
are involved in this process, and only one of them average more than
50 people on Sunday mornings. These types of transformation opportunities are available to churches of every size.

Independent churches can call upon consultants to help them
with their diagnostic process. Small churches will immediately claim
that they cannot afford outside consultants, but not all consultants are
expensive. Besides, most independent churches are not completely independent. They usually have a network of churches with whom they
relate, and the consultant could be a veteran, respected pastor from
one of those churches. Small churches can often call upon a nearby
seminary and find a professor who would help them identify areas
that are keeping them from being healthy. Many colleges and universi-
ties have leadership departments, and someone from those departments might be available to assist. Many resources are available for the
church that's serious about wanting to be healthier.

Once the diagnostic process has been completed, the church will
have to decide how to address any issues that are identified. One of
the worst mistakes the church can make at this time is to try to deal
with too many problems at once. Small churches don't have the resources to attack every problem at once. Addressing too many issues at
the same time will lead to frustration, will likely result in none of the
issues being corrected, and will cause the church to give up and return
to its unhealthful patterns. Focus on one area and determine how you
can improve it. Once you have that area corrected, then you can turn
your resources over to another one.

The key is to determine which area will give you the greatest return. An accident victim is taken to a hospital emergency room with a
punctured lung and assorted scrapes and cuts. The doctors there won't
worry about cleaning up those scrapes and cuts until they address the
damaged lungs. The patient could die while they're putting Band-Aids
on the minor cuts. Like the doctors in the emergency room, your

church will have to determine what the most important issue is that keeps your church from being alive and healthy and then focus your attention on correcting that one thing.

Focus on Your Strengths, Not Your Weaknesses

It's also important that you focus on your strengths and not your weaknesses. As Marcus Buckingham and Donald O. Clifton write, "You will excel only by maximizing your strengths, never by fixing your weaknesses."[6] This does not mean that you should ignore weaknesses. Find ways to manage your weaknesses, but concentrate on maximizing your strengths.

As an area minister, I'm in a different church nearly every week. One of the things I notice is how the church greets people, especially visitors. Most of the churches do at least an adequate job, but some come across as very unfriendly or at least uninterested that someone new has joined them that Sunday. Assuming that these church members are friendly folk who have simply not been taught how to welcome guests to the church, I believe this is an area that could be quickly addressed. Here's an example of some nice people—a strength—who just need some training in how to greet people. Doing so would be maximizing a strength of the church. By the way, this is not an unusual example. Many people who serve as church greeters could use a little instruction in how to properly greet people.

Look for Systemic Issues

Unhealthy churches usually believe their problems are programmatic in nature. If they had better leadership, better facilities, or better resources, they could solve their problems. If they attend conferences, it's to seek the latest program that's sure to fix their problems and put them on the road to health and growth. Tom Bandy perfectly describes the thinking that exists in too many small churches:

> The experts who have the most impact on the declining church board are always those with the most practical tips to resolve the issues here named. The declining church board is only interested in *programmatic* change. It is never interested in *systemic* change. In other words, board members want the experts to give them tips, keys, ideas, or programs that will help the existing *system* of church life work more effectively. It is always best that the tips or programs not cost too much *financially*, but it is crucial that the tips or

programs not cost too much *psychologically*. The basic system of the church must be preserved.[7]

Of course, the problem of preserving the present system is that your system is perfectly designed for the present results you are seeing.[8] We are told that one definition of insanity is believing that we can keep doing the same thing over and over again and get different results. The fact is that if we keep doing the same things, we will continue to get the same results. If the church is not healthy and growing, it is because the present system does not promote health and growth. The only way the church can regain its health is to change the systems that prevent health. Renewing the church is not enough. We need nothing less than church transformation.

Church Transformation Does Not Happen Overnight

An unhealthy body did not become unhealthy overnight. Our bodies are impacted by years of eating habits and levels of exercise, stress, and abuse. Unhealthy churches also do not suddenly become unhealthy overnight. Years of poor leadership, dysfunctional systems, and a lack of vision contribute to the present-day problems many churches are now experiencing. Just as an unhealthy body cannot be healed overnight, an unhealthy church will not be quickly healed either. It takes time to undo the effects of years of unhealthy patterns. Bill Easum tells us,

> If you're in an unhealthy church, take a 20-year view of the situation. Realize that it will take several years to build a core of spiritual leaders. Cast your vision for a healthy church. Begin to work with the few who respond and nurture them in a small group as long as it takes. In the interim, work hard to get a few of the disciples in "official" places to make the process of decision-making easier. Move forward as the opportunity arises.[9]

If you are the pastor, this means that you need to be willing to make a long-term commitment to remain at your church. This will be addressed in more detail in a later chapter, but the normal one- or two-year pastorate in a small church is not enough to effect any kind of transformation. In fact, another short-term pastorate will probably make the problem worse.

This also requires intentionality on the part of the leadership. We must be intentional in seeking persons who can provide transformational leadership in our churches, and we must be intentional in nurturing and developing them. We must be diligent in seeking opportunities to transform the church system and be ready to move quickly when those opportunities present themselves.

Summary

If your church is not currently healthy, it can become healthy again. It won't happen overnight, and it won't be easy, but it can happen. You need to properly diagnose the problems and determine their causes. After the diagnosis, the church must determine what issues to focus on first. What will give you the greatest benefit for the time and cost invested? Remember to concentrate on your strengths. Develop your strengths, and find ways to manage around your weaknesses. Look for systemic problems, not programmatic problems.

Church transformation is the key, not renewing old systems that no longer work. Commit yourself to taking the long-term approach. You did not become unhealthy overnight, and it will take time to regain that health. Begin the healing process in your church, and take advantage of opportunities as they present themselves.

The Importance of a Proper Theology and Doctrine

The theology of a church will have a greater impact upon the future health of the church than will all of the church's programs and strategies.[1]

—Glenn Daman

Everything must have a solid foundation on which to build. In this book we examine several aspects of church life that contribute to its health, but there has to be a foundation that supports each of these aspects. For the Christian and for the church, that foundation is a good theology and doctrine.

Glenn Daman reminds us that a church's theology impacts everything the church does. Although a church may function in many different ways, it's essentially a theological organism that exists to transform people's lives so those lives reflect Jesus Christ. A faulty or weak theology will result in a weak church unable to bring about that needed transformation.[2]

We have become a nation that has abandoned absolute truth. Postmodern people have no problem believing contradictory truths. Once a person has abandoned absolute truth, absolute morals are also abandoned, and ethical and moral issues are determined by the circumstances of the moment. The church is not exempt from this dilemma. As a result of his years of studying the church, George Barna challenges us:

Think about the Christian church in the U.S. Spiritual anarchy is rampant. People wholeheartedly believe things that are antithetical to what the Bible teaches—and nobody challenges them or

26

imposes sanctions on them for their beliefs. In fact, we have become so theologically complacent that nobody really knows what anyone else believes because we're too busy doing our own thing. We cannot really call the faith of American Christians a Bible-based faith. It is a synthetic, syncretic faith.[3]

In his letter to young Timothy, the apostle Paul predicted this would happen: "Now the Spirit expressly says that in latter times some will depart from the faith, giving heed to deceiving spirits and doctrines of demons, speaking lies in hypocrisy, having their own conscience seared with a hot iron" (1 Tim. 4:1-2).

Many churches are in trouble today because they've abandoned their theological and doctrinal roots and displaced the teachings of Christ. No church that does this can be healthy regardless of how successful it appears to be. Churches can build beautiful structures and create exciting programs, but without a solid foundation, those structures will collapse and the programs will fail.

This summer three houses have been built around our home. It's amazing how fast skilled people can build a house, but I noticed that all three of them spent a great deal of time ensuring the foundation was right before proceeding to do anything else. Building a ministry is no different than building a house. Jesus warned in a parable that to build a house on the wrong foundation would lead to the loss of that house (Matt. 7:24-27). The place to begin is at the foundation, and the foundation of the church must be a proper theology and doctrine.

It's not the intent of this book to provide you with a clear, systematic, biblical theology and doctrine, of course. Many excellent resources are available to the pastor and layperson to help them with these. However, while there are issues of theology and doctrine that can be debated and discussed, I believe there are some basic firm beliefs that cannot be abandoned:

- The Bible is fully inspired by God and the definitive authority in all things necessary for salvation (2 Tim. 3:15-17).
- Humanity was created in the image of God in order that we might have a relationship with God. As a result of humanity's choosing to disobey God, that relationship was broken (Gen. 1—3).
- God sent His Son, Jesus Christ, to the earth to restore the relationship between God and humanity (John 3:16).
- Jesus Christ was born of a virgin (Matt. 1:18-25), died on a cross (Matt. 27:45-50) as the propitiation for our sins (1 John 4:10), and rose again on the third day (Luke 24:1-7).

- Jesus Christ is the only way by which a person can know God (John 14:6).
- Because we have all sinned and disobeyed God (Rom. 3:23), each of us needs to turn to Christ and receive the gift of eternal life (Rom. 6:23).

Each element in this brief outline must be studied to fully understand its implications for how we live and how the church conducts its ministry. Our churches will never be healthy until we do this. As Charles Colson and Ellen Santilli Vaughn write, "To be the church—our highest calling—depends on understanding the very character of the body of Christ on earth. Only then can we understand what it means to live as the people of God, serving God in today's world."[4]

Biblical Preaching Is Critical

In the small church the pastor will have the primary responsibility of teaching sound theology and doctrine to the congregation. Larger churches can offer their members a wide variety of learning opportunities through small groups and specific classes. These opportunities usually don't exist in the smaller church. The primary opportunity for teaching sound theology and doctrine to the small church is usually during the Sunday morning worship time. This means that the preaching ministry of the small-church pastor is critical if the church is to be sound in its beliefs.

John MacArthur Jr. writes, "The decline of preaching is a major factor contributing to the church's weakness and worldliness. If the church is to regain its spiritual health, preaching must return to its proper biblical foundation."[5] MacArthur feels so strongly about this that he stresses that "no man's pastoral ministry will be successful in God's sight who does not give preaching its proper place."[6]

One of the first things I do when I visit a pastor is to look at the library in his or her office. I'm often shocked by the small number of books on those shelves and how few of them are theological and doctrinal in nature. Most of the books are the popular self-help books. I have to wonder what feeds this pastor's preaching.

Many small-church pastors lack formal seminary training. This would seem to make it even more important that they invest in some good theologically and doctrinally sound commentaries and other Bible study aids. We can't consistently feed our congregations sound doctrine and theology if we're not studying the Scriptures to understand what God is saying to us.

It's not enough to just be able to exegete scripture; we also have to exegete the culture we're seeking to teach. People don't want to know simply what the Bible says; they also want to know how that message applies to their lives. I call it the "so what" principle. When I complete a sermon, I put myself in the place of my listeners and ask, "OK. That's what the Bible says—but so what? How can this impact my life this week? What difference will this message possibly make as I return to my world Monday morning?" If the sermon doesn't pass the "so what" test, my work is not complete.

Our sermons also have to be understandable to our audience. Speaking "churchese" to people who were not raised in the church will not be effective. Speaking to issues that are not the experience of our listeners will make it hard for them to understand and apply what they hear. Jesus often used examples from the rural countryside because His listeners could identify with them. They understood shepherding and sowing seeds. Today many people would not benefit from such examples because they have no experience with rural living. Ron Martoia clearly understands this:

> Faithfully translating the biblical message into the language of our culture is our primary job. The message remains the same by impacting the understanding of the target audience the same as it impacted the original hearers. This requires creative translation: not a retranslation of the biblical text, but a translation of the way we communicate it in a culture that is constantly changing. In other words, we must be both exegetes of Scripture and exegetes of culture. If we read Scripture carefully without reading culture, we have an important message that's not understood. If we read culture carefully, but fail to communicate the biblical message, we've been relevant but for no reason. Both biblical and cultural exegesis are necessary for effective postmodern ministry.[7]

Some churches have mistakenly believed that if they teach doctrine in their churches, they'll be unable to reach the unchurched in their communities. They fear that the solid preaching of the Bible will be offensive to these people, so they water down their messages to make them more appealing to more people.

This thinking is wrong for a number of reasons, and it's also inaccurate. Thom Rainer is the dean of the Billy Graham School of Missions, Evangelism, and Church Growth at Southern Baptist Theological Seminary in Louisville, Kentucky. After two years researching formerly unchurched people, he reached a significant conclusion:

One important lesson we learned from the formerly unchurched is that we should never dilute biblical teachings for the sake of the unchurched. . . . Ninety-one percent of the formerly unchurched indicated that doctrine was an important factor that attracted them to the church.[8]

Sunday School

Sunday Schools used to be a primary means of teaching sound doctrine and theology, but these are not well attended today in many churches. Many churches report that fewer than half of those who attend worship services attend Sunday School. Further study would probably find that many of those attending Sunday School are children, especially in unhealthy churches. Tom Bandy tells us that "in the declining church system, less than 1 percent of the adults are involved in any planned faith development or spirituality group during the week."[9]

The focus in recent years has moved away from discipleship to church growth. We've put our resources into reaching new people, but we've done a poor job of helping them grow spiritually. The bulk of church resources that do go to the Sunday School program are often earmarked for the children's classes, while adult programs are largely neglected. The smaller church is especially prone to doing this because they have few resources, and the mind-set is that the children are the future of the church.

The problem with that thinking is that the church needs leaders today, and we're not doing a good job of helping these new adults develop a sound doctrine and develop into the spiritual leadership our churches need. One denominational leader recently told me about one of their larger churches that was experiencing tremendous growth but was seeing a steady decline in the numbers attending Sunday School. As these new members were beginning to assume positions of leadership and responsibility in the church, the church was having significant problems.

These people don't understand their denominational history and heritage, and they have not developed a sound doctrine. They apply marketplace solutions to spiritual problems because that's all they know. This leader said he feared for his denomination as this pattern is being repeated in many churches. The need for spiritual leadership is addressed in a later chapter, but the basis of spiritual leadership is having a sound, biblical theology and doctrine.

Small churches that want to be healthy have to find a way to strengthen their Sunday School program or find other ways to involve adults in a regular study of the Bible. Many churches may need to completely revamp their educational methods and find new, creative ways of exploring Scripture that will appeal to adults.

One small-church pastor I know spends each summer preaching expository sermons through a book of the Bible. Another pastor has changed the format of his church's Sunday evening service and made it into a Bible study time with more discussion than is normally seen in a traditional service.

For too long we have moaned about the biblical illiteracy of our congregations. We need to stop talking about the problem and begin addressing it. The health of our churches absolutely depends on our having a proper theology and doctrine. Without a sound biblical theology and doctrine upon which to build, none of the other items discussed in this book will lead your church to health.

Summary

Without a solid foundation, a building will not stand. This is also true for churches. For a healthy church, this foundation must be sound theology and doctrine. While there are areas in which good people can disagree, there are also beliefs that are essential to the faith, and the church must not deny them.

In the small church the primary opportunity for teaching sound theology and doctrine is during the pastor's sermon. The second most effective time is during Sunday School. Unfortunately, many churches report decreasing Sunday School enrollment, especially in their adult classes. These adults are the leaders and future leaders of the church, and if they're not instructed in sound theology and doctrine, the church will not maintain its health. Churches must find ways to strengthen their teaching ministries if we want our members to be more theologically and doctrinally sound in their beliefs.

4
The Value of a Vision

We must keep dreaming and keep visioning to keep our churches, ministries, and personal lives from perishing.[1]

—Dan Southerland

A church without a clear understanding of God's vision for its ministry is like an octopus on roller skates. There may be a lot of activity, but it's not going anywhere. Without a commonly understood vision, everyone in the church has his or her own vision of what the church should be doing. When these visions collide, and they will, problems develop, and ministry comes to an abrupt halt.

Sometimes I'm asked to meet with a church that's in conflict. One question I always ask people in those churches is "What is this church's common vision?" People usually respond with a confused look or by honestly answering, "We don't have one." In most cases, they have just identified the root cause of their conflict.

What Is a Vision?

"A vision is a clear mental picture of what could be, fueled by the conviction that it should be,"[2] writes Andy Stanley. Vision often comes out of dissatisfaction with the current state of affairs. Perhaps one of the best vision stories in the Bible is the story of Nehemiah. When he heard about the state of Jerusalem, he wept and sought God. He had a clear image of rebuilding the city and the walls around it and the belief that they should be rebuilt. That vision gave him the courage to ask the Babylonian king for permission to return to his homeland and rebuild the city and wall. Despite the obstacles, he and his followers rebuilt the wall in only 52 days (Neh. 6:15).

One lesson we learn from Nehemiah is that a vision doesn't make life easier. In fact, it often makes life more difficult. According to Thomas G. Bandy, "A church gripped by a vision will never be the same again. A vision may be a joyous experience, but it is never a pleasant experience. A vision never eases the stress of a congregation; it always multiplies the stress of congregational life."[3]

Nothing is easier than continuing the status quo. Nehemiah may have been a slave in a foreign land, but he was the king's cupbearer. He could have lived out his life in the royal court relatively free from stress and problems. But when he caught God's vision, his life would never again be the same. He would face challenges and obstacles that would nearly overwhelm him. As he looked at the rubble that had once been Jerusalem, he must have questioned his ability to rebuild it. His enemies made the task even harder. Without a clear vision from God, he might not have had the courage to continue, but that vision sustained him, as it does all visionary leaders, through the difficult times.[4]

While living in a rut may make life easy, it will also lead to death. It has been said that a rut is nothing but a grave with the ends kicked out. There's not much life around a grave, and there's not much life around a rut either. A vision will lead a church out of its ruts, but it will also challenge the church as it has not been challenged in a long time.

Lyle Schaller tells us that "Without a vision of a new tomorrow, we are all inclined to attempt to do yesterday all over again."[5] Without a new vision, churches and individuals will remain in their ruts doing the same things again and again wondering why nothing ever changes. But when people buy into God's vision, exciting things begin to happen. Old comfort zones are left behind as new opportunities are embraced, and new life is experienced by those who participate in God's vision.

Vision Provides Focus

Nehemiah would not be distracted by the challenges of his enemies or the difficulty of the task. The apostle Paul would not be kept from Jerusalem despite repeated warning from his friends that he was facing danger (Acts 21:4-14). Jesus could have called upon angels to deliver Him from the Cross, but He chose not to do so because He understood the will of God for His life (Matt. 26:53-54). Each of these men was focused in fulfilling what he understood to be God's vision for his life.

A healthy church is focused in its ministry. Too many churches are attempting to be everything to everybody, and they wonder why they fail to ever accomplish anything of significance. A church going through conflict recently called in a consultant to help it find a solution to its problems. Among other things the consultant suggested that the church do the following:

- Drastically reduce the number of its committees.
- Discover God's clear vision for its ministry.
- Strategically use its members according to their spiritual giftedness to fulfill that ministry.

Unfortunately, the church refused that counsel. The people could not believe they were asked to reduce the number of their committees. After all, they had always had them. As a result, the active members of that small church continue to be worn out from trying to do too many things, most of which add nothing to the ministry of the church or to its surrounding community.

Small churches need the focus that God's vision for their ministry can provide. They have neither the people nor the financial resources to be everything to everybody. This means that some good things will be left undone so that the most important things can be accomplished. Bill Hybels writes,

> Every vision that is cast embraces essential activities, but it also excludes activities that may be good in and of themselves, but if they are unrelated to the specific vision of a particular church, pursuing them will do more harm than good. Nothing neutralizes the redemptive potential of a church faster than trying to be all things to all people. It is impossible for one church to do it all.[6]

Bill Hybels is the pastor of Willow Creek Community Church, a true megachurch in the Chicago area. Yet he believes that no one church can do it all. Why do many small churches not understand they can't do it all either? We struggle and struggle doing things that God has no longer called us to do and wonder why we aren't more successful. If we would only take the time to discover God's present vision for our churches, we would find ministry to be not only easier but also more successful, because we would be focusing on simply doing what God is calling us to do.

Vision Unites the Church

God's vision has the power to unite the church. Those who followed Nehemiah could have decided to pursue their own agendas, but they didn't. They had bought into the vision God had given Nehemiah, and they were united in their efforts to rebuild the wall and city. They were focused on a common purpose that they completed in an amazingly short period of time. It's astounding what a church that's united around a common purpose can accomplish.

For 20 years I served as the bivocational pastor of a church in Indiana. Near the end of my time there, the church determined that they needed a new fellowship area. We spent the next two years praying, planning, and trying to buy some additional land adjacent to our property. Although we were unsuccessful in buying the land, the church determined that God was leading us to build this new facility. An architect drew up some plans based on what we told him we wanted in our building. He estimated it would cost about $250,000. This seemed like a lot of money to a congregation that averaged about 50 people on Sunday mornings, but we decided to go ahead with the building.

Some men in the church had construction experience, so the church members were able to do some of the work themselves. Contractors were hired to do the work the members were not comfortable doing or did not have the expertise to do. For the next two years the church united around the task of constructing this building. Some worked on the facility nearly every Saturday and occasionally during the week. Several women volunteered to bring food to the workers. People gave financially to the project. Children helped with cleanup. The final cost was a little under $200,000 due to the church members doing so much of the work. The truly remarkable thing is that the building was completed debt-free. The church never had to borrow a dime on this project.

I can tell this story because I resigned from the church to accept my present ministry position shortly after the foundation was completed. The church's achievement had nothing to do with me—it had everything to do with their clear understanding of God's vision for their church. United around a common purpose, the church built a top-quality facility that will serve them well for many years. Because the church has no debt on the building, it can concentrate its finances on ministry to the community.

Vision Enables People to Move Beyond Their Own Self-Interests

Changes in a church are often difficult when people believe that the change may not be in their own best interest.[7] Without a vision of a preferred future, the personal cost may appear to be much greater than any possible gain. It's understandable that people will resist change in such cases.

We're in the midst of a worship war in many of our churches. Some people prefer one type of music and worship style, while some prefer other styles. Some churches have gone to blended services, in which they try to combine different types in one service. Sometimes this works; sometimes it just upsets all the people half the time! Other churches have gone to two or more worship services each Sunday, with different music and styles in each. Small churches often struggle with what to do, because their size makes it difficult to have more than one service.

I recently heard a story about a pastor who wanted the church to include more contemporary music. He laid the groundwork in some sermons prior to the business meeting in which the vote would be taken. He tried to stress how this change might help them reach some younger people the church had not been reaching.

At the business meeting the pastor presented his reasons for changing the worship service. He knew that the church would not make a decision on this matter until the church patriarch stated his position. When the pastor finished, every eye was on the patriarch as he slowly stood to his feet and announced that he did not like the style of music the pastor was proposing to include in their worship services. For two or three minutes he explained why he did not like that music. Then he paused for several seconds and said, "But if we don't do something different, my grandson is going to die without God. I vote we make the changes the pastor has proposed." The pastor breathed a sigh of relief as the man slowly began to sit down—and then rose back onto his feet and announced, "But I'm not going to sing those songs!"

This patriarch was willing to put his own self-interests aside for the hope of reaching other people for Christ. He would not allow his preferences to get in the way of fulfilling God's vision for the church.

Vision Allows the Church to Be Proactive Rather than Reactive

Without a vision, a church will usually spend its time responding to situations rather than proactively shaping its future.[8] Church leadership will be reduced to constantly fighting fires in the church while never finding time to lead its people in ministry.

In addition to being a minister, I also own a small heating and air-conditioning business. A common theme that small business owners constantly hear is that we must be careful not to work so much *in* our business that we have no time to work *on* our business. Many of my competitors began as service technicians who wanted their own businesses. After starting their own companies, they continued to do the service work. In addition, they found they also had to do payroll, pay the bills, order parts and equipment, schedule, handle complaints, and do all the other unseen things that must happen for a business to exist. They never find time to develop a business plan, a marketing strategy, or continue their training. Like a hamster in the wheel, they run faster and faster but go nowhere. Unable to grow, their companies either close or continue to exist at a much lower level than they're capable of attaining. This occurs because they spent their time working *in* their business rather than working *on* it.

Doesn't this sound like many churches? Without a compelling vision, we remain focused on the circumstances going on around us. Granted, we often do have to respond to some of these circumstances, but if that's all we do, we'll forever remain stuck in the ruts we've created for ourselves.

Vision gives us something else on which to focus. It allows us to focus on the preferred future God has for us. It challenges us to pray and plan how we can achieve the things God has given us to do. It helps us develop sermons that will shape the future of the church as we challenge our people to rise up to the challenges God has put before us. It helps our committees and boards focus on the future.

Why Many Small Churches Lack Vision

If there are so many benefits to a vision, why do many small churches continue to operate without one? We've already discussed how small churches resemble families, and most families don't have a vision for their family. They usually prefer to live day-to-day unless something unusual occurs. Very seldom will a family sit down and write out their dreams for the coming year. Small churches are the same way. While most members hope their church will do well, few will ever seek God's vision for their church and determine how they can achieve it.[9]

Hope is not a strategy that's likely to lead to a successful ministry. Drifting along from Sunday to Sunday will probably not produce the kind of ministry the church is capable of experiencing. God has a vision for even the smallest of churches, and the churches that earnestly desire to be used by God will seek that vision and find ways to implement it.

The Source of the Vision

In the smaller church, vision is unlikely to come from the pastor unless he or she has been there for several years. In fact, it may be counterproductive for the pastor to begin promoting his or her vision for the church. Small-church pastors must not try to force their vision upon the church. Their role is to facilitate the vision process as the people begin to seek God.[10]

Many small-church pastors destroy their ministries prematurely by trying to impose their sense of vision on their churches. They're so caught up in their own ideas that they fail to value the history and tradition of what was there before them. They also fail to understand the importance of community and continuity in the small church.[11]

It's much better to develop a vision team.[12] These are individuals who will pray together, talk to people both inside and outside the congregation, and seek to understand God's will for the church. Until the vision is clear, this will be the most important work occurring in the church, and only the best persons should be on this team.

This will not be an easy task. Leith Anderson describes the process that often occurs when seeking a vision: "Most visions come from a lengthy process of learning, praying, observing, brainstorming with others, trial and error, rough drafts, trial balloons, false starts, refinements, partial agreement, eventual adoption, and incremental implementation."[13] In other words, discovering God's vision is hard work, but as we've seen, it's work that produces great rewards.

Communicating the Vision

Determining God's vision for the church is only the first step. Now it's essential that this vision be communicated to the rest of the church in such a way that they'll take ownership of it. A congregation will not unite around a vision until they own that vision. They might agree that the proposal is a good one, but that's not the same as their taking ownership of a vision. Too often a pastor takes the smiles and nodding heads of the congregation as acceptance of a vision he or she is sharing. In many cases, the people are just agreeing that this sounds like something the pastor should do. Unless they accept ownership of that vision for themselves, they're unlikely to be involved in the execution of it.

In the sharing of the vision, there are some mistakes to avoid. The first is to assume the congregation understands the vision the first time it's communicated. "In the excitement to announce the vision and begin implementation, change leaders often forget that the rest of the congregation has not been a part of the intense dialogue and soul-searching that are a part of discerning and articulating the vision. In forgetting this key fact, they underestimate the amount of communication that will be required."[14]

Visionary leaders are sometimes surprised that people don't get excited about a vision the first time they hear it. We probably should be more surprised if they do, especially if the vision is suddenly thrust upon them from on high. Wise visionary leaders understand that the sharing of a vision is best done as a dialogue and not a pronouncement. Conversations with our congregations about their lives, hopes, and dreams about the future provide the best opportunity to share a vision.[15] In those conversations the leader can help people see and feel the vision and demonstrate how they can live out that vision in their lives now and in the future.[16] This helps ensure that these individuals will share in the ownership of the vision, which means that they'll be involved in its implementation.

Repetition is another key element of communicating the vision. Rick Warren states that "vision and purpose must be restated every twenty-six days to keep the church moving in the right direction."[17] I often failed to do that in my early days as a pastor. As a result, we would begin some good things, and then we would get sidetracked by other items needing our attention. Sometimes we never regained our focus, and visions were left unfinished. Dan Southerland explains why this happens:

> The drift is always downward in the vision process. That means we tend to drift away from our defined purpose, target, and strategy. We forget what it is that we are doing, who it is that we are trying to reach, and why we are doing it this way. People need to hear a vision again and again until it becomes a part of their soul. They need to hear it until it becomes their vision—and then they will still need to hear it so they won't forget.[18]

Reactions to the Vision

It's a frightening thing to receive God's vision. Old Testament prophets were always reluctant to give God's vision to the people. Moses gave God one excuse after another why he should not be the one to approach Pharaoh about letting the Israelites leave Egypt because of his fear of how the Israelites and the Egyptians would respond: "But suppose they will not believe me or listen to my voice; suppose they say, 'The LORD has not appeared to you'" (Exod. 4:1). Jeremiah tried to back out because of his youth (Jer. 1:6). Isaiah declined because of his sinfulness (Isa. 6:5). None of these great men of God initially believed he was worthy to declare God's vision to His people.

Each of these men was rejected by some who refused to accept the vision God had given them. Jesus experienced the same rejection. The disciples witnessed many miracles at the hand of Jesus, and yet they often found His message hard. We read, "From that time many of His disciples went back and walked with Him no more" (John 6:66).

There are some things a church leader needs to understand, and one of them is that some people are going to leave your church no matter what you do. Some want to experience new ways of doing ministry. They're seeking a fresh vision from God, and they're committed to following God's guidance. Others are content with the way things are, and the last thing they want is a visionary leader who will mess up their nice, comfortable little church.

If you seek a fresh vision from God and attempt to lead the congregation to fulfill that vision, some folks will leave. If you choose to remain stuck in the ruts, others will leave. Accept the fact that some will leave. As the leader, if you set the vision and stay the course, you will determine who will leave.[19]

Unfortunately, many of our churches are more interested in maintaining harmony in the church than they are in ministry.[20] This is especially true in smaller churches due to the importance of relationships in those churches. Families prefer harmony to chaos, and family churches are no exception. A new idea will quickly be rejected in the small church if it will possibly upset the delicate harmony existing in the church. We'll explore this in more detail in the chapter on change, but we need to understand that this will be part of the church's reaction when a fresh vision is being communicated.

This does not make for a healthy church. Peace at any price is not worth it. It's not a healthy church if some individuals are given veto power over any new idea that's proposed.

In a healthy church a vision can be discussed. The congregation can pray together to seek a clear understanding of what God might be saying. People can disagree with aspects of the vision without becoming disagreeable. The congregation is not railroaded into accepting the vision but is given time to understand it and decide if this is truly the direction in which God is leading.

In a healthy church people don't believe that a vision can come only from the pastor. In fact, a vision might even come from someone outside the church family. It may be heard in the words of a former member who left because of some problem that exists or existed in the church. A vision might first be voiced by a new member of the church who has noticed something that the long-time members could no longer see.

A healthy small church will continually seek a fresh new vision from God. It understands that God is always calling His Church to minister to the present world, and that ministry will change as the world changes. Although a church might wish to live in its comfort zone, a healthy church knows that God has not called the Church to be comfortable but to minister to the world for which Jesus Christ died. Understanding God's vision for your church will equip you to do that.

Summary

Vision is absolutely essential for the healthy small church. It enables the church to better focus on the ministry God has given it, unites the church, and reduces the potential of conflict. Vision also helps the church look beyond its four walls to the needs of those in the community. Many churches spend their time and energy simply reacting to events around them; vision challenges them to become more proactive and provides them the opportunity to shape their own future.

Despite these benefits, many of those in small churches refuse to invest the time and effort it takes to discern God's vision for their churches. They hope something they do will produce good results, but they never spend time determining what God would have them to do.

It's vital that the church seeks God's vision for the church—not the pastor's vision nor the vision of the lay leadership but God's vision. While that vision may come from someone in leadership, it may also come from a person on the fringe of church life or even from outside the church family. It may come quickly, but often discerning God's vision takes much time and prayer.

Once the vision is known, it must be communicated to the congregation so they can begin to understand it and take ownership. Such ownership is vital for the success of the vision and usually requires numerous times of communicating the vision in a multitude of ways.

Not everyone will respond positively to God's vision for the church. Vision often calls for change, and this can be very unsettling to the smaller church. There will be questions about how these changes will affect the church, and especially how they will impact the individuals who have dedicated their lives to this congregation. Some may choose to leave the church due to the direction the church is moving. While this is unfortunate, church leaders need to understand that some people are going to leave the church regardless of what the church decides to do.

Healthy churches will always be seeking a fresh vision from God. They'll celebrate when they accomplish a great task, but almost immediately they'll begin seeking a new vision so they can continue to have an effective ministry to their communities.

5
Transformational Worship

*The reason the small church can have a great
worship service is because it does not require a worship
team, a musically talented song leader, a dynamic
preacher, or a gifted pianist. All that is required
is a sincere and pure heart before God.*[1]

—Glenn Daman

A larger church may focus on cell groups, programs, or specialized ministries, but the small church is centered on its worship service. This is the time when the church family comes together, when they can share their joys and sorrows of the past week. They often recognize birthdays and anniversaries, wedding announcements are made, and thanks are given for cards received during a recent hospital stay.

Most important, of course, the worship service is the time to experience God, an opportunity for people to allow God to restore order to their lives after spending the past week in the rat race of life. We often joke about our church members sitting in the same pews each week, but this is one way they reorder their lives. That pew is often the only place in their world that is not changing. It is here they feel secure and accepted. This is the place where they encounter God, and they leave the service confident that God will go with them back into the chaotic world in which they live.

Because the worship service is so important to the small church, we need to spend the time necessary to ensure that those who participate have the opportunity to experience God. One pastor of a fast-growing church recently told me that he and his volunteer staff spend approximately 40 hours a week preparing the worship service for the next Sunday. Other people in that church take care of the pastoral care needs. Few small church pastors have the staff, the time, or the resources to invest that much time in preparing the worship service. However, select-ing the hymns an hour before the service and going into the worship service with no real plan isn't an option for a healthy church either.[2]

The Purpose of Worship

The purpose of worship is to express our praise and thankfulness to God. We acknowledge His presence in our lives, and we give Him thanks for the blessings we've received from Him. Each element of the worship service should direct our focus toward the God who created us and who sustains us by His grace. Our worship services would take on a much different flavor if we remembered that God is the audience of our worship.

However, there's another aspect of worship that we often miss. Jack Hayford reminds us that "worship is an opportunity for man to invite God's power and presence to move among those worshiping Him."[3] Eddie Gibbs expresses this truth in a slightly different way: "Worship focuses on the God who is not only *there* but also *here* among us."[4] Worship is not only for God but also for the worshiper. We are re-minded when we worship that we serve a God who has promised nev-er to leave us in the difficult times of our lives (Heb. 13:5).

The story is told of a small child who could not sleep one night due to a terrible storm and asked her mother to sleep with her. Her mother refused and reminded her that God was with her and would protect her. The little girl thought about this for a moment and re-sponded, "But, Mommy—I need someone with skin on them."

People are no longer interested merely in hearing about God—they want to *experience* God. They want to be intimate with the Holy. They want to feel God. Leonard Sweet states it clearly when he writes, "If postmodern worship can't make people furiously *feel* and *think* (in the modern world the church made people only 'think'), it can't show them how God's Word transforms the way we 'feel.'"[5]

Worship should enable people to experience God in real and sig-nificant ways. We live in a rapidly changing time, and many of us don't appreciate many of the changes. Stress levels are high as we rush around trying to satisfy all the demands on our time. Many people deal with unbelievable amounts of loneliness and pain. New uncer-tainties entered our lives by the terrorist attacks of September 11, 2001. Minorities and women continue to face the realities of racism and sex-ism. Like the little girl, we cry out for a God with skin—someone we can experience.

Donald Miller, a professor of religion at the University of Southern California, studied what he called new paradigm churches. In his research he reports,

> Many people told us that in the act of worshiping, they find their defenses and pretenses of everyday life vanish. They said that in communing with God, who knows the secrets of the human heart, feelings and emotions surface that are otherwise buried. Sometimes they get in touch with deep wounds inflicted by others; other times they return to personal failures that have been rationalized and repressed. Connecting with these memories and feelings and giving them to God for healing are important byproducts of worship.[6]

People will be drawn to these types of worship services in which they can experience healing and transformation in their lives. Thomas Long is correct when he writes, "People are not hungry for more worship services, for more hymns, sermons, and anthems. They are hungry for experiences with God, which can come through worship; in the most primal sense, this hunger is what beckons people to worship."[7]

What are the characteristics of such experiential, transformational worship services? How do we provide the types of worship opportunities that will be most meaningful to the people who enter our sanctuaries? Are we willing to pay the price that may be associated with such worship? These are important questions that every church leader interested in worship renewal must ask.

The main responsibility for worship renewal in the small church will be on the pastor. Some pastors don't see the need to change anything about their worship services. Others are not willing to deal with the problems that such changes might cause. Pastors have told me that they will never change anything about their worship services, and if people don't feel they can worship there, they can go elsewhere. These churches are likely to continue to offer a worship experience that was relevant in the 1950s but has little meaning to people in the 21st century.

Characteristics of Transformational Worship

Music is the cause of much church conflict today, so we might as well begin by looking at music. Rick Warren warns us that "once you have decided on the style of music you're going to use in worship, you have set the direction of your church in far more ways than you realize. It will determine the kind of people you attract, the kind of people you keep, and the kind of people you lose."[8]

Some churches sing nothing but the old standard hymns. These have several advantages. They're generally well known to church members who find comfort and meaning in them. Most, but not all, have sound theology. Many of them teach powerful faith lessons we need to learn and remember.

But one primary disadvantage that older hymns have is that many of them are sung at a much slower tempo than most people prefer today. This is not so much the fault of the hymn writers as it is of those leading the singing. Many can be sung at a much faster tempo. I remember singing "We're Marching to Zion" in a church once and thinking, "These people would *never* get to Zion at *this* pace!" They weren't marching—they were crawling. Such hymns are meant to be sung with exuberance and joy—so don't drag them out.

Another disadvantage to some hymns is the archaic language they use. How many people know what "Here I raise mine Ebenezer" means? The King James English used in many hymns is also a turn-off to many people. Some of these songs have been rewritten for the newer hymnals to reflect more modern English. These hymnals would be a good investment for the church that prefers the older hymns.

Some churches now sing nothing but praise songs set to contemporary music. These are often easy to learn, and many have a great impact on worshipers and lead to a more exuberant style of worship, often with clapping. Slower songs are often sung with eyes closed and hands uplifted.

But contemporary songs also have weaknesses, of course. Some are rather shallow, sometimes referred to as "7-11" songs—with 7 words that are repeated 11 times—with little if any theological content. Their main value is in the emotions they raise in the worshipers and the fact that younger people can often better relate to them.

Worship wars are being fought over styles of music, and that's sad. The particular style of music is not what's important. There's no right or wrong style of music. The important thing is whether or not people are encountering God.

Last night I attended an associational men's meeting. The program for the evening was led by one of the pastors in that association who played the piano and sang. During part of his program he demonstrated how hymns could be played Floyd Cramer style. After the service, one retired individual remarked, with tears running down his cheeks, how one song in particular touched him.

In another setting this program might not have been so meaningful. Many younger people might not even know who Floyd Cramer was or his contribution to music. The pastor understood his audience and brought a program that was meaningful to everyone who attended. We truly experienced God in that setting.

Understand the People

This leads us to a second aspect of transformational worship. Relevant worship begins by understanding the people and matching the worship experience to the culture. Eddie Gibbs explains that "worship is always contextualized so that no one style should be regarded as normative or more spiritual than another. What turns on some people is likely to put off others."[9]

I enjoy Southern gospel quartet music. My wife and I are permanent seat-holders at the National Southern Gospel Quartet Convention held each year in Louisville, Kentucky. We go all six nights of the convention.

A good pastor friend of mine would not walk across the street to hear that type of music if someone gave him a free ticket. Instead, he enjoys Christian rock music. What he would consider a good worship experience, I would consider noise.

Worship planning must consider the context of the people who attend the church and those the church is hoping to reach. I know one pastor who has studied the county in which his church is located and found that a country music station is the station most listened to by people there. The music in that church reflects that preference.

Of course, there are other aspects of the worship service besides music. Times of prayer, the sharing of testimonies and prayer concerns, how the Lord's Supper is observed, the way the offering is received, whether or not an invitation is given after each service—all must be done in a way that will be meaningful to the worshipers.

Acceptable methods of worship also vary from church to church. It's becoming more common to hear people applaud after a musical presentation, but I've been in churches where that's not acceptable. Uplifted hands are also more common in worship services, but there are other churches where such expressions of worship would be out of place. Many people like to clap while singing more upbeat songs, but this is also not acceptable in some churches.

When I preach about worship, I like to point out the many ways people worshiped in the Bible and give people permission to worship in similar ways. I like to clap to music, and if I feel moved to do so, I'll lift my hands in praise of God. I encourage people to worship in a way that's meaningful to them. My purpose is not to get them to lift their hands or to clap or dance. My purpose is to give them freedom to worship in such a way they are most apt to experience God.

By the way, when I'm in a church I know does not approve of expressive forms of worship, I refrain from worshiping in those ways. I respect the context in which I'm worshiping, and I don't want to be a hindrance to someone worshiping God.

I mentioned earlier that worship planning must consider the people who attend the church and those the church would like to reach. This is very hard to do, especially in the smaller church. In many churches there are four or five generations to consider. These generations often have very different preferences when it comes to music and worship styles. Whose preferences should be considered first?

As mentioned earlier, some churches have tried to blend their worship services to include all preferences. Done well, this can be a good solution to a difficult situation. But as also noted earlier, it can lead to everybody being mad half the time too! I think a better solution in most cases is to offer two worship services that have specific targets. Consider these words from Bill Easum:

> Two styles of worship are needed in congregations that have reached their plateaus or are declining. Aging congregations cannot be expected to give up a style of worship that fits their culture in order to reach the younger generations. Neither is it fair to ask the younger generations to worship in the culture of the older generation. It is much easier to start a separate and distinct worship service.[10]

Even in the small church the idea of two worship services makes a lot of sense. For one thing, it helps protect the church from the worship wars that are tearing apart too many churches today. "It is very difficult for many Christians to comprehend that their meaningful traditions mean little or nothing to another person—Sunday worship, hymn singing, baptism, communion, church membership, altar calls, recitation of the Lord's Prayer, or singing of praise choruses."[11] This is why these battles are so fierce at times. People are trying to protect a heritage that has no meaning to others.

A traditional service can be offered that will have meaning to the long-time members of the church, and an alternative worship service can be offered to those who would find more meaning in a different format. Again, that format would be determined by the people the church was seeking to reach. However, suggesting that two services be offered in a small church will raise several objections.

- *The limited resources of a small church will make it difficult to offer two services.* Difficult yes, but not impossible. If new people are recruited to help lead the second service, this will result in growth of the church before a second service is even started.
- *We won't know the people in the other service.* That might be true, but which is more important: knowing everybody or reaching people for the kingdom of God?
- *We won't feel the sense of family with the people in the other service that we've always felt with just one service.* This is a valid concern because of the strong sense of family in the smaller church. However, this can be addressed by having events in which people of both services come together for meals and fellowship.

While these might be the objections that are voiced, there may be an unspoken objection on people's minds—the fear that if their worship is transformed, God's power might be manifest in a way they can't control.[12]

We saw in the beginning of this chapter how important it is for people to have some routine in their worship service. Transforming worship can be very threatening to that sense of routine. Besides, most Christians have heard stories of churches that have begun practices that don't seem right. Their desire to protect their church from excess causes them to resist any effort to transform their worship services. The wise worship leader will address this concern at the beginning of any attempt to transform the worship experience.

The Right Focus

A third element of transforming worship is to help people focus on God. Most adults attend worship services thinking of themselves and their situations. They must focus their attention on God before they'll be able to worship Him.

Consider a common scene on Sunday morning. The family gets up a little late. Breakfast is a hurried affair. People can't find the clothes they wanted to wear. A button is missing. Just as the family is going out the door, a child announces the need to go to the bathroom. Rushing around makes everybody a little edgy, and sharp words are spoken back and forth. They speed down the road and arrive at the church two minutes before the service begins. They take their seats just as the prelude begins, and now they're expected to worship.

This humorous example happens often, but many of these problems can be resolved with a little planning on Saturday evening. Other examples are not so amusing and are more difficult to overcome.

How does a woman worship God on Sunday when her husband told her a few days earlier that he was leaving her? How does a mother of young children worship when she's expecting crucial medical test results the next Tuesday? How can a man worship God when he was told Friday that his company was downsizing and that his services would no longer be needed? How does a father worship when he found out a few days earlier that his child was using drugs? The list goes on and on.

In a healthy small church these people are given permission to share their hurts and fears. Instead of being judged, they're loved as their church family gathers around them in support. The worship service is changed to allow healing to begin in the one who is hurting. Doesn't Jesus say that when we reach out to the hurting, we're reaching out to Him (Matt. 25:34-45)? Isn't such a loving response to those who are hurting an act of worship to our Creator?

Experiment with Worship

Change occurs very slowly in a small church. The wise leader doesn't change the worship service all at once but instead invites the church to experiment with different formats and different music styles. People are much more willing to accept a temporary change if they know they can always go back to the familiar if it doesn't work.

The experiment should not be limited to simply changing a song here and there or altering how the announcements are made. Do something completely different. One year we had "Biker Sunday" at our church. We invited motorcycle riders from the area for a special service. I invited a friend of mine who had been a tough biker before he met Jesus Christ to come and share his testimony. He presented a powerful story, telling how God had changed his life and led him to work with the Christian Motorcycle Association as well as his own personal ministry. I led the service dressed in jeans and a tee shirt and wearing my riding boots. My motorcycle was parked out in the parking lot along with those of our visitors. Several bikers attended and expressed their appreciation at our service. Incidentally, this was the second highest attended service we had that year. Only on Easter Sunday did we have more people attend the worship service. I think people came just to see what would happen!

Sally Morgenthaler tells the following story of a church that did something completely different one Sunday and the success they enjoyed.

A small congregation in a small Midwestern town decided to enlist the help of two teenage boys who had dropped out of the church a few years before but who had great video skills. Church leaders asked the boys to create a video about God's faithfulness in 95-year-old "Aunt Clara," who is now living in a nursing home. It was to be presented to the church for an All-Saints Day service. This was a church that had never done any form of video projection before; the boys had to travel 45 miles to rent a projector. They assembled a video collage of photos from the 100-year-old history of the church and interspersed them with various shots of Aunt Clara. After they put it together and showed it to the congregation, the unanimous response was, "Why haven't we done this before?" So they did the same for Mother's Day.[13]

Worship with Joy

Few things are more discouraging than joyless worship. Some worship leaders obviously don't want to be leading worship. They probably agreed to do so because no one else would. They simply announce the number of the next hymn and tell people when to stand up and sit down. Because they don't sing out, the congregation mumbles its way through the songs. Their lack of enthusiasm is mirrored by the congregation making the worship experience an ordeal rather than the exciting opportunity it should be.

Worship is coming into the very presence of God. Ps. 100:1-2 reads, "Make a joyful shout to the LORD, all you lands! Serve the LORD with gladness; come before His presence with singing." Consider Ps. 98:4-6: "Shout joyfully to the LORD, all the earth; Break forth in song, rejoice, and sing praises. Sing to the LORD with the harp, with the harp and the sound of a psalm, With trumpets and the sound of a horn; Shout joyfully before the LORD, the King." Nothing in these or any other such verses suggests a dirge as we approach God.

Our worship services should be times of joy and celebration. Laughter and excitement should be experienced in worship. Let's stop baptizing people in lemon juice and alum! This does not mean that we become frivolous and refuse to show God proper respect. We must never forget that we're coming before a holy God, but let's also not forget that He has said in His Word that we should approach Him with joy and gladness.

Select as worship leaders people who want to lead worship. Give people permission to worship God in ways that are meaningful to them. Make the worship experience a time of celebration and joy. It will transform the lives of the people and the life of your church.

Healthy small churches understand the importance of worship, and wise leaders invest the time into preparing a worship experience that will be meaningful and bring people into contact with God. A church without a vibrant worship service can't be a healthy church. It doesn't take a lot of money or talent for this to happen. All it takes is people who sincerely want to worship God and who desire to see others share in that experience.

Summary

Worship is important in the small church because it's the one time when the church family comes together to share their lives and to celebrate God. It's a time when people seek a new, fresh experience with God. For these reasons, transforming worship requires preparation on the part of the pastor and other worship leaders.

Music is an important part of worship. The type of music used in worship services has caused many church battles in recent years. While this is unfortunate, it's understandable, because different music appeals to different people. Many long-time church members find the hymns of the faith meaningful to their worship, while younger persons may find a more upbeat style helps them better connect with God. Each church will have to decide how best to provide a worship experience that speaks to both camps. Receiving permission to experiment with the worship service will be the best way to determine the most effective worship service experience for your congregation.

More important than style is the joy created in worship. This should be a joyful, exciting time. Selecting worship leaders who enjoy leading worship is critical to having an exciting, uplifting worship experience. Worship that enables people to connect with God results in changed lives, and such changes will always produce joy.

6

Acceptance of Change

While quantitative research shows that 61 percent of all worshipers report that they are ready for their congregation to try something new, qualitative research reveals that many members will accept the new thing only if it is in their own self-interest or not too different from what they already have.[1]

—Jeff Woods

The story is told of a small church that realized it needed to construct a new building. The church appointed a committee to study the matter and make a recommendation to the congregation. At a church business meeting several months later, the committee gave a recommendation to build the new facility. The debate continued over several more business meetings of the church. Finally, the congregation voted that they would
- build a new church building;
- build the new building on the same site as the existing building;
- use the materials of the old building to build the new facility;
- continue to meet in the old building until the new one was finished!

Unfortunately, this example describes how some churches approach change. They fear change, and unhealthy churches fear it the most. It's one of the great ironies of church life that churches that need to change the most are the least likely to change. They would rather die than change.

Small-church leaders should expect that few people will be excited about any proposed change when they first hear about it. Herb Miller explains why:

A national study by *American Demographics* magazine reported that 47 percent of Americans are highly resistant to change. Another 17 percent of Americans are peace lovers. They do not actively resist change, but they prefer that no one rock the boat. Who do the 17 percent side with when someone suggests a change? The vocal 47 percent that strongly resist change, of course. Result: Expect 64 percent of governing-board members and church staff to vote against a new idea the first time they hear it.[2]

Why People Resist Change

There are many reasons that people resist change. For some people change is an admission of failure. They've invested their lives in doing church a certain way, and change means that way no longer works. They'll argue that "things will return to normal if the church can simply continue to do what it has always done but in greater quantities or with superior quality."[3] Such churches will try to work harder and challenge their members to be "more committed." A common complaint in such churches is that their members simply aren't as committed to the church as they used to be.

What these well-meaning folks forget is that their precious way of doing ministry was once someone's new idea that replaced a method that was no longer working. People change, and times change. The church must be willing to replace existing ways of doing church that are no longer effective in reaching today's culture.

Some people resist change because they realize the new church will be different from the old one. Like an old pair of shoes, the church they've known for so many years is comfortable. All organizations, including churches, prefer routine and the status quo. Pastors and lay leadership can perform their duties with minimal resistance and stress. They'e not confronted with the challenge of learning anything new.[4]

As we mused earlier, living in a rut is easy, but it's still nothing more than a grave with the ends kicked out.

A third reason people resist change is more personal. In the old church system they knew their role. They're not sure what their role would be in a changed church or if they would even *have* a role. It can be a real power issue. A man was approaching his fifth anniversary as the pastor of a church when some of the lay leaders told him he should probably be looking for another church since none of their previous pastors stayed there more than five years. They ran that church and didn't want a pastor to stay too long who might be able to take some of their power. In another church, newer members were kept out of decision-making roles by the older members who didn't want to relinquish their power.

Fortunately, for most people this concern about roles is not about power. It's about their Christian identity. They've served this church for years, and much of their identity is wrapped up in this service. They know how to teach a Sunday School class, or they thought they did. Now it's suggested that there might be other ways, better ways, to teach a class. The pianist has played in the church since high school, and now it's being recommended that other instruments besides a piano should be part of the worship service. After all these years of faithful service, do they still have a role in this new church? It's no wonder they're frightened by change.

Churches that have a rapid pastoral turnover often are resistant to change. Some small churches may have a new pastor every year or two. When a change is suggested, the church automatically rejects it, because they believe that by the time the change is instituted, the pastor will leave and they'll be stuck with the change. Besides, the new pastor will probably want to do something else different. To protect themselves, they automatically reject any change that's proposed.

A fifth reason churches may resist change is that they don't believe the change will make any difference. These churches have been in decline so long that the people have essentially given up. They circle the wagons to protect the meager assets they have so the church can last as long as possible. As long as they can pay someone to preach and keep the utilities paid, they'll be satisfied.

The final reason is that churches often don't see the *need* for change. They don't believe there *is* a problem. These churches will often talk of things they wish were different, such as more young adults or youth attending the church, but they fail to see that their present church systems are responsible for the way things are. Again, they complain about a lack of dedication or the multiple opportunities for people to do other things on Sunday besides go to church. They may complain about the new community church that offers multiple ministries that draw the people away from their church. Such people never see that the problem may lie in their current church system. Because they're blind to their own responsibility, they don't see any reason to change anything.

What Needs to Be Changed

Every church is different, so it's impossible to address any specific thing that should be changed in a church. However, after 20 years of pastoring a small bivocational church and working with multiple churches in denominational work, I can make some suggestions for your church to consider.

The worship services of many small churches need to be speeded up. Not every announcement has to be read or explained, especially if it's printed in the bulletin. If people are going to speak from the platform, they should be seated on or near the platform. There's no reason for them to wait until they're introduced and then slowly walk down from the back pew to make their announcement. People have been conditioned by television and other activities to expect things to move at a more rapid pace than they experience in many churches, and this expectation should be considered when planning the worship service.

In the previous chapter we addressed the music in the worship service. It bears repeating that the music you use in your service will largely determine the people you'll attract to your church. If your church is not attracting the people it wants, you should take a careful look at your music.

Are the times of your worship services convenient for people? Many of our churches have met at a certain time for decades, and those times have never been reviewed. One men's group was used to meeting at 7:30 P.M. For years people complained about the time of the meeting because it caused the men to get home late in the evening. Nothing was done until it was finally pointed out that the time was set many years ago when most of the participating men ran dairy farms. The later time was convenient for them because it allowed them time to finish their milking. The problem was that no one who attended the meeting now had farmed for years. When the men agreed to move the starting time to 7:00, more began to attend. Our worship times should not be set in stone. If people find other times to be more convenient, your church should consider them.

Is every committee and position in your church necessary? In smaller churches it's not uncommon for people to serve on several committees in a church in addition to teaching a class or serving in some other capacity. Often a committee may exist simply because it's always existed in the church. It might be possible to eliminate some committees and free up the members for more actual ministry. One church had a missions treasurer in addition to its regular treasurer. The missions treasurer would send the church's mission offering to the denomination each month. When the church realized that for many years the missions treasurer merely picked up the check from the church treasurer and mailed it, they eliminated the position of missions treasurer and enabled that person the opportunity to do more constructive ministry.

If your church is ready to genuinely consider some changes, it might think about eliminating all existing committees. That will sound like blasphemy to some, but it's actually very workable. Some churches have been very successful at replacing their committees with ministry teams. When people ask me the difference, I explain that committees *talk* about ministry, and ministry teams *do* ministry.

One church of several hundred members eliminated their committees and replaced them with two ministry teams. One team focuses on the physical ministries of the church, and the other team is responsible for the spiritual ministries. Everyone in the church was allowed to select which team he or she wanted to serve on, and no one was allowed to be on both teams. This church is nearing its third year with this structure, and they never want to return to their old committee format.

Is the church ready to receive guests? Is the building clean and accessible? Are there signs to clearly point people to classrooms, restrooms, nurseries, and other facilities in the church? Is each person greeted by someone who enjoys that ministry and has been trained in how to do it correctly? I am in many churches each year, and as noted in an earlier chapter, not every greeter should be allowed to greet people until he or she receives some training.

How much do people have to know before they can participate in church events? A notice in the church bulletin reads, "The women's mission circle will meet at Jean's house this week at the usual time." Is there only one Jean in the church? Just exactly where is her house located? What's the usual time of this meeting? What day do they meet? What will happen at this meeting? Written and oral announcements must be user-friendly if the church wants people to understand them and participate in the events.

Do the sermons lift up or *beat* up? After several years in the pastorate, I began to realize that my sermons had become more negative and critical. I did not intentionally prepare sermons that were critical, but I did intentionally determine that my sermons would become more positive and uplifting. To make myself accountable to the congregation, I confessed to them one Sunday that I realized I had become rather negative from the pulpit and that I was making a conscious decision to preach more positive and helpful sermons. I promised them they would never have to be afraid to bring their unchurched friends and family to church. I found I could preach the same message from a positive perspective as easily as from a negative one and that people responded to the positive ones much better.

These suggestions are given only to help you think about the changes that might be helpful to your church. Through prayer and observation, you'll identify the issues that need the most attention in your particular church.

How to Bring Change to Your Church

Begin by taking a long-term approach. According to Clay Smith, "Significant changes in the life of a congregation usually take three to five years to put into place."[5] One of the biggest mistakes leaders make is to try to hurry the process. A change leader must understand that people are being asked to give up something that has great meaning to them, and they can't be forced to do this before they're ready. Failing to understand this will likely mean that the change will not happen, and the change leader's ministry in that church may well be shortened.

Start small. Small changes are more easily accepted than big changes. "The most effective change processes are incremental; they break down big problems into small, doable steps and get a person to say yes numerous times, not just once. Successful leaders help others to see how progress can be made by breaking the journey down into measurable goals and milestones."[6] People who might object to a major change will often accept these smaller steps. When they see that the small changes benefited the church, they often have the confidence to accept bigger challenges.

John Maxwell talks about the power of momentum. He believes that "with enough momentum, nearly any kind of change is possible."[7] Momentum comes from achieving successes. A basketball team appears to be beaten, but then it scores a couple of baskets. Suddenly the team is energized. Its members become more aggressive on defense and offense. Their fans are on their feet cheering every play. They may score 10 or 12 unanswered points. The momentum has shifted, and these team members who had been hanging their heads begin to play like champions. What does the coach of the other team do? He calls a time-out to break their momentum.

When small-church leaders introduce change slowly and break it down into small steps, the people can accept it. The successes of the small changes make it possible to keep introducing change. Rather than being frightened, the people are excited and energized by the victories they're seeing. It's often difficult to get momentum started in a small church, but when you get some momentum, it will enable great things to happen.

Leaders of change must learn how to help people process their feelings during the change process. "People do not resist change, per se. People resist loss."[8] The church as they know it will be no more as it begins to change, and the members will mourn that loss. There is grief and pain that must be managed. Jeff Woods tells us that "'change management' often becomes 'pain management.'"[9] This is another reason why it's important to make incremental changes rather than sweeping changes. However, some people will experience pain with even the smallest of changes. Expect it, and be ready to minister to that pain.

Members of the congregation must be helped to understand that the changes will be beneficial to the church. John Maxwell correctly says, "People will not change until they perceive that the advantages of changing outweigh the disadvantages of continuing with the way things are."[10] Margaret Wheatley agrees when she writes, "Change is prompted only when an organization decides that changing is the only way to maintain itself."[11]

Perhaps an example outside the church will help. For years we've been told of the dangers of smoking tobacco. Even some tobacco companies are now running advertisements warning people of the risks associated with tobacco. Most people, including smokers, acknowledge those risks. Yet millions of people continue to smoke.

Many of these smokers have tried numerous times to quit, but they always go back to smoking. Frustrated, they can only say that it's much harder than they thought. The pain of stopping smoking is greater than the possible gains they might enjoy if they stopped, so they continue to smoke.

Suddenly, however, for one smoker a visit to the doctor's office changes everything. A test is questionable. The diagnosis is not good. The doctor has the smoker's full attention when explaining that the smoking must stop immediately if the smoker wants any chance of seeing his or her children grow up. Despite repeated past failures, the smoker is able to stop smoking. It's not easy, but now the gain is well worth the pain.

Acknowledge the pain that will come with the change, but help the people understand that the gains will be well worth it. Enable them to see the future of the church after the changes are implemented. This powerful picture will enable many to accept the changes.

In an effort to encourage us to buy their products, companies will often try to make us dissatisfied with what we currently have. Effective change leaders will use the same strategy. In order to bring about change, it's often necessary to deliberately cause the congregation to be dissatisfied with the current state of the church.[12]

Small churches are notoriously complacent. The family atmosphere of a small church creates a sense of satisfaction. Although there may be talk of wanting to do some new thing, there's seldom any concentrated effort to do so. Ministry shortcomings are glossed over by reminders that, after all, they're just a small church with limited resources. Nothing changes because most people are satisfied with the current state of the church.

Creating dissatisfaction in the church will probably lead to conflict, but it's absolutely necessary if change is to be successfully introduced into the church. Along with that dissatisfaction, there must be a sense of urgency regarding the change. The church cannot afford to spend the next decade discussing needed changes. Change leaders must clearly state what will happen to the church if the needed changes are not made.

Jim Herrington, Mike Bonem, and James H. Furr state in their book, "Urgency is critical in the individual congregation. It creates a driving force that makes the organization willing to accept change and to challenge the conventional wisdom. It is no wonder that so many churches seem unwilling to change—they lack any sense of urgency."[13]

John Kotter claims that the biggest mistake people make when trying to introduce change into an organization is failing to establish a high sense of urgency.[14] Although he writes for business organizations, his warning applies to small-church pastors as well. "A good rule of thumb in a major change is *Never underestimate the magnitude of the forces that reinforce complacency and that help maintain the status quo.*"[15]

How can a sense of urgency be developed in a church?

- Expose key leaders of the church to other churches that are doing a particular ministry well. Give those leaders an opportunity to talk to pastoral and lay leadership of those churches to hear what inspired them to focus on that ministry.
- Invite an outside leader to an open forum of the church to talk

about the future of the church. Members can be encouraged to share their perceived strengths and weaknesses of the church as well as their own vision for what they would like to see the church become in the next five years. I recently met with one of the churches I serve, and there was some excellent discussion about the present situation of the church, the desired future, and some things it might take to get there.

- Most of us like to tell inspiring stories of transformed churches that began exciting ministries that led to great growth. However, we also know churches that refused to change and died. Those stories need to be told as well. God is under no obligation to breathe life into a church that refuses to follow Him.

Politicians often leak information to see what type of reaction they'll get from the public. Although they may complain about leaks, they use them to "test the waters." Change leaders in the church should also leak information about what changes they're considering. These leaks should be made to those who will most likely support the change. This gives these individuals an opportunity to ask questions about the change and make suggestions that might improve the change. It also gives them time to talk among themselves. By the time the suggested change is made public, many of these people will already be supportive of the change and will help persuade the rest of the people.

I've written elsewhere about the need for the small-church pastor to identify the true leaders in the congregation. It takes a pastor many years in a small church to earn the trust of the congregation. Without that trust, it's very difficult for the pastor to introduce significant change to a church. However, if that pastor can influence those in the church who influence others, those lay leaders can be valuable allies. If they buy into the recommended changes, they can influence others to accept them as well.

When encountering resistance to changes, try a trial period of a few weeks or months without making a permanent commitment. Most people are willing to try something for a few weeks. After the trial period, the church leaders can examine the results of the trial and make recommendations regarding permanent change.

Change Is Necessary

We live in a rapidly changing world. Our churches must learn to change quickly if we wish to minister to the world in which we live. As John Maxwell says, "When you're through changing, you're through."[16]

A church's ministry has ended when it refuses to minister in the present. A healthy small church is committed to relevant ministry, and that church knows that regular change will be necessary if it's to remain relevant. It will readily accept some changes, while others will be more difficult, but the healthy small church will change so it can continue to provide a viable ministry to the community God has given it.

Summary

Change is inevitable if a church wishes to remain relevant to its culture, but many small churches are very resistant to change. Change impacts the comfort that people have come to expect in their churches. It's a threat to their well-being, because it might impact the roles they've had in the church. Other churches simply don't believe change will make any difference, and they would prefer to protect what they have left rather than take the chance on losing it to some change being proposed.

When change is accepted, it won't happen overnight. Significant change can take years to implement. It's usually best to start with small changes that offer the best opportunity for success. Such success will give people courage to try greater changes. Change is better accepted when people feel an urgency to make the suggested change. Wise leaders will create this sense of urgency when proposing change to the church.

7
The Ability to Handle Conflict

Then the contention became so sharp that they parted from one another. And so Barnabas took Mark and sailed to Cyprus; but Paul chose Silas and departed, being commended by the brethren to the grace of God.

—Acts 15:39-40

Church conflict is nothing new. Even in the first-century Church we find examples of conflict among the church leaders, between the Hebrews and the Hellenists in Jerusalem over perceived differences in the treatment of their widows (Acts 6:1), and between the circumcised and uncircumcised converts (Acts 15:1-2). Not only should we not be surprised when conflict occurs in our churches, but we should even welcome that conflict as a normal part of growth. Peter Stenke writes, "For any system to be healthy, it has to be challenged; sometimes that challenge comes in the form of conflict. A healthy congregation is one that actively and responsibly addresses or heals its disturbances."[1]

It's appropriate that this chapter follows the chapter on change. Any effort to promote significant change in any organization will provoke conflict. This is especially true in the smaller church that is so tightly knit together. Effective church leaders will anticipate the conflict likely to develop and will have plans to manage that conflict before they even introduce the change to the church. John Maxwell refers to this ability as "the Law of Navigation."[2] Not every leader has this ability. Leaders often find themselves surprised by the conflict that occurs, and their efforts to bring about change fail because they were not prepared for the conflict.

Unfortunately, conflict management and resolution is not taught in many seminaries. Pastors and other church leaders have to learn these skills on their own, often in the midst of the conflict. With the knowledge that conflict is inevitable in churches, it makes sense that church leaders would learn some tools to help them deal with it before it occurs.

Causes of Church Conflict

There's no way a single volume could cover all the possible causes of conflict in a church, but some common things often create it, such as stress, pride, fear, and poor leadership.

Stress is often at the root of conflict. It may be caused by the church, or its cause may be outside the church, but the conflict that results is often brought into the church. According to Larry L. McSwain and William C. Treadwell Jr., "Often the church is the first social grouping to experience the dysfunctions of persons living with unconquered stress. Behaviors of anger, hostility, frustration, hurt, and distance are signals of need that call for response and care."[3]

Interfamily problems will have an effect on a small family church. We've already seen how some small churches can be composed primarily of people who are related. If there's stress in the family, it will find its way into the church. The stress of a divorce can bring that conflict into the church especially if the family is divided in their support of each partner. The loss of a job may be devastating to a family, and the resultant stress can result in church conflict.

In the small church the stresses may be between two of the primary families who make up the church. Church conflicts have erupted because two farmers with adjoining properties had a boundary dispute. Teenagers of two families date one another, and a church conflict develops because of the circumstances of their breakup. The possibilities for intrafamily conflict are endless, but it's almost certain that those conflicts will find their way into the small church.

Of course, the stress may be due to events within the church. As already discussed, the stress of a major change will cause at least some measure of conflict in the church. A person may feel he or she was overlooked for a position in the church and that his or her talents are not appreciated. Someone else may become upset because the church does not take a strong position on some matter about which he or she feels great passion. It should be noted that it doesn't take a major event to cause some people to feel stress. I know of a family who left a church because they felt their children did not have an appropriate role in a church musical program.

Another emotion that often results in church conflict is pride. In fact, Bob Russell, pastor of Southeast Christian Church in Louisville, Kentucky, writes,

> The number one cause of division in churches today is pride. People become proud of their influence and status, so much so that when you threaten their little seat of power, they will come out fighting. They will pretend they have the church's best interests at heart, but the real issue is a matter of *who's in charge*.[4]

Pride can show itself in many ways in church. Someone might be offended when he is not asked to serve in a certain position in the church, especially if he has served the church in that capacity before. Another person becomes upset when she is not invited to sing a solo in the Christmas program. A third person believes that the pastor spends more time with another family in the church and ignores hers. The list of possible offenses is endless.

Many churches have that special person who's always right and is ready to share his or her opinion with everyone on every issue. This person's opinion is the only one that matters. The church stays in a state of conflict because of this person's overbearing ways. Because of the sense of family in the smaller church, such a person is seldom challenged. The church walks on egg shells around him or her rather than risking a confrontation. In doing so, the congregation becomes increasingly unhealthier. Bob Russell challenges churches in this situation:

> Putting up with a divisive person in the church to avoid problems is like putting up with a cancerous tumor without operating to avoid the pain of surgery. You must operate so that it can continue to be alive and healthy. If your church is to continue winning souls and transforming lives, you must maintain harmony. That occasionally means that a difficult operation must be undertaken by the leaders.[5]

Fear is another cause of conflict. Many small churches have adopted a survival mentality, especially the ones that have been in existence for many years. They have become used to barely getting by, and they really have no hope that things will ever get better for them. Their congregations are often older. If their church members lived through the Great Depression, they may be very careful to not overextend their resources. Some of the members are simply hoping this church they have attended all their lives will exist long enough to bury them. Any suggested

change is met with alarm and fear. They fear the church's limited resources will be lost in some new effort that certainly won't work any-
way. Any attempt to move ahead with the change will lead to conflict.

There is also the fear of embarrassment or pain. A small church
once developed a special ministry that was very successful. However,
an incident occurred that brought both pain and embarrassment to
the church. The ministry was abandoned. Years later, someone who
did not know about the previous incident suggested the church do
something similar. The response was both immediate and negative.
People remembered the earlier problems, and they feared the results
would be the same. The person wisely dropped the idea, or serious
conflicts would have developed in that church.

Poor leadership, poor planning, and poor implementation are
more causes of church conflict.[6] Although pastors are always willing to
blame the congregation for the church's problems and its lack of forward motion, I learned early in my pastoral ministry that I was often
my own worst enemy.

Having a clear vision is not enough. The church leadership has to
think through the planning and implementation of that vision. Again,
this goes back to John Maxwell's Law of Navigation. How can we take
this vision through to implementation? What obstacles are we likely
to face? Who are the people we need to get on board? How do we
clearly communicate the vision to the congregation? What are the
processes we need to follow to help the church make a decision regarding this idea?

A church should be as concerned with the process of reaching a
decision as it is regarding the decision itself. Excluding members from
the process invites conflict. People might agree with the decision but
feel uncomfortable with the process that was followed. Even if conflict
is avoided in such situations, seeds of distrust might be sown that can
cause later problems.

Dealing with Conflict

Since conflict is inevitable, church leaders need to have a plan of
action for dealing with it. Perhaps the most important thing that
needs to be done is to refuse to pretend the conflict does not exist.
"The best way to manage conflict is to treat it as something normal
and bring it out into the open where it can be handled fairly and con-
structively."[7]

A healthy church is one in which the stresses that are being experienced within it can be acknowledged, discussed, and appropriate action taken with respect to them. There must be some commonality of perception about the nature of the church, its goals, its ministries, and its responses to persons in need if a management of stress is to occur. If unspoken expectations can be surfaced in a process of open communication, unrealistic hopes can be moderated before stressful situations result in a failure of the church to respond appropriately.[8]

This is not easy to do in the family structure of the small church. Too often we're willing to accept peace at any price. In the words of Tom Bandy, we prefer to be a "cult of harmony."[9] He writes, "Traditional organizations are designed to pursue the Holy Grail to be 'one happy family,' recapturing the supposed unity of the culturally homogeneous village church with the white steeple on top."[10] Unfortunately, refusing to admit the conflict makes the church unable to resolve it and prevents the church from the opportunity to move beyond it.

Once the church admits it has a conflict, the next step is to determine if the conflict is based upon personalities or principles. Keith Huttenlocker writes,

> Personality-centered conflict results from a basic dislike of one person for another. The feeling is often mutual—eventually if not initially. . . . Whether it is between church members or between the church pastor and church members, personality-centered conflict has its basis in prescriptive expectations. Someone is unwilling to allow another to be different.[11]

Churches are made up of people with very different personalities, and sometimes those personalities will clash. The best resolution to such a conflict comes if one of the parties is mature enough to realize what's happening and is willing to back down.

If neither party is willing to back off, it's often helpful to bring in an outside mediator to resolve the conflict. The pastor of a small church can't win if he or she tries to resolve the conflict between two strong-willed people. No matter what options the pastor proposes to the combatants, he or she will be seen as taking one side against the other.

If the conflict is between the pastor and church members, it's important for the pastor to stay calm. Pastors don't like conflict, and most of us don't like to be challenged. "The first instinct of most leaders is to respond defensively when challenged," states Jim Van Yperen. "It is always the worst response. In conflict, never confront power with power. Always confront power with truth."[12]

In one small church some church members challenged the pastor over a decision the church had made. They believed the pastor had unduly influenced the decision, and they had concerns about the process that had been followed. People asked for appointments to meet the pastor to discuss their concerns. They wanted to know if he believed proper procedures had been followed and if he had unduly influenced church members to reach the decision.

In fact, the pastor had not been aware church members were going to make the recommendation that led to that decision and was quite angry that his integrity was being called into question. However, instead of reacting emotionally to their accusations, he met with each person who requested a meeting and simply answered them truthfully. He treated each accuser with respect, acknowledged his or her concerns, and answered questions.

He also wisely did two other things. First, he did not ask the supporters of the decision to yield to a vocal minority and back away from the decision. Second, he did not try to short-circuit the conflict. He correctly believed that the conflict was not really about him or the decision. The conflict was really about what the church was going to be in the future.

This church was at a crossroads. This decision would determine whether or not the church would continue the forward movement it had enjoyed in recent years. The pastor understood that "conflicts, at their root, consist of differences in fervently held beliefs, and differences in perspective are the engine of human progress,"[13] in the words of Ronald A. Heifetz and Marty Linsky. This conflict was necessary for the church's continued transformation.

Although there were heated words exchanged between people in this small church, the decision held, and the church did continue to grow. Nobody left the church despite some early threats to do so. The church learned a number of lessons from this experience, including the fact that conflicts don't have to tear a church apart.

Prevention is the best way to avoid conflict. Sometimes the best approach to personality-centered conflict is to keep the people apart as much as possible. It's better if some people are not allowed to serve together on the same committees or work on the same ministry teams. Even if the people share similar interests and gifts, it would be far better to give each of them separate opportunities to use those gifts. In Acts 15 we read about a conflict between Paul and Barnabas. The end result was two mission trips rather than one. That is not a bad ending to a church conflict.

The conflict may not be about personalities but about dearly held principles. Keith Huttenlocker defines these types of conflicts:

> Principle-centered conflict . . . results from sharp differences of opinion over matters of significant importance to the opposing parties . . . [It] often occurs when someone feels compelled to promote something, rectify something, or preserve something. When the conflict becomes full-blown, there is a lot of blaming, judging, and labeling. Combatants may be especially ruthless with one another because of the presumed righteousness of the cause.[14]

Such conflict may focus on justice issues such as capital punishment, or moral issues such as abortion. Theological issues can lead to principle-centered conflict. Replacing the pews in the church with more modern chairs can lead to this type of conflict, as some people will want to preserve the décor of the church facility. Resolving such conflict is very difficult, because each side is convinced that God is on their side. Backing down is seen as compromising one's principles, and few people are comfortable doing that.

Many church conflicts are about neither personalities nor principles—they're about power. Who will control the church? Tom Bandy suggests that 20 percent of a church may consist of controllers.[15] He writes of these people: "They want the church to prop up their lifestyles and service their personal interests. They want the power to tell people what to think, how to behave, and what to do."[16] They will strongly resist any change that might threaten that power.

> Controllers do not want to grow and do not want anyone else to grow. That is why they limit continuing education budgets and obsessively hire professionals to do as many ministries as possible. Personal and spiritual growth imply change, and change leads to instability, and instability inhibits the Controller's goal to share congregational life around his or her personal agenda.[17]

A church locked in a power struggle is a church that is going nowhere. For too long, small churches have given controllers virtual veto power over every proposal. A large majority of the church might favor a suggested change, but if the controller opposes the suggestion, it will never happen. This unhealthy behavior means that the church will never effectively minister to its community and ensures the ultimate demise of the church.

Small churches always approach such conflict with a fear that people will get angry and leave the church. Unfortunately, the truth is that the church is already losing people. It's losing those who want to see the church change, grow, and more effectively minister to its community. It's also losing those potential new people who are spiritually hungry and seeking God but can't find Him amid the power struggle in the church.

All you need to ask is: "Do you love controllers more than your own children, parents, neighbors, and work associates?" Is it more important to keep controlling clergy, matriarchs, patriarchs, wealthy trustees, or domineering institutional managers, rather than welcome your own teenagers, parents and immediate loved ones into the community of faith? The choice may be as profound as "Christ or Institution," but for most people it is as simple as "Controller or my teenager." If one must go so the other can belong, what will be your preference?[18]

These are painful questions for the small church, but these are questions a church that wishes to remain healthy must answer. Few people enjoy the type of confrontation that's necessary to resolve and manage conflict, but such confrontation can't be avoided. Conflict seldom goes away on its own. In fact, if ignored, conflict will usually intensify. That's why conflict must be addressed quickly, calmly, and with integrity.

Resolving Conflict with Integrity

Regardless of the intensity of the conflict and its precipitating cause, there should exist for all of us a standard of conduct that will not be violated. Both pastors and laypersons should be governed by a system of personal ethics that prevails over the systems of conflict whenever the two come into confrontation. . . . Both are mandated to act with integrity.[19]

Allow me to close this chapter with a suggested standard of conduct for congregations involved in a conflict situation. These apply equally to pastors and laypeople.

- *Respond quickly to problems when they first begin to appear.* In a conflict situation, time is not an ally, and indecision about whether or not to act will almost certainly cause the conflict to escalate. Seldom will things get better if you ignore the problems.
- *Speak directly to the persons with whom you have a disagreement.* This is biblical (Matt. 18:15). Too often we want to tell everyone else. This does nothing but escalate the conflict. A situation that could be easily resolved between two people becomes much more difficult to manage when others are brought into it.

- *Maintain confidentiality.* What's told to you in private must stay private. Breeching confidentiality is a serious integrity violation.
- *Refuse to listen to gossip.* If people come to you wanting to "share something that's on my heart," stop them the moment you realize that this is nothing but gossip. Simply tell them you prefer to not listen to such things unless the other person is present. That will usually stop the gossiper. I recently told two churches embroiled in conflict that the best thing some of the people could do would be to unplug their telephones.
- *Treat one another with respect.* Even if there are strong differences between you, each person has deep feelings about this matter. Those feelings deserve respect. Christians should be able to disagree without being disagreeable.
- *Don't have a hidden agenda or unspoken concerns.* Each party must share openly and honestly with one another if they desire to resolve the dispute.
- *Remember that the kingdom of God is more important than your agenda.* If you realize that the majority of the church does not share your belief about a matter that's critically important to you, be mature enough to find another church that's more in line with your beliefs.
- *Be willing to submit your conflict to a third party.* Sometimes an outside mediator can present solutions to a situation that others don't consider. However, don't wait until the matter is a full-blown crisis before requesting help. Consultants are seldom asked to assist until the conflict has reached at least a stage-three conflict in which people are more interested in winning than in resolving disputes. In a stage-one conflict people are talking and resolving differences. A stage-two conflict escalates to the point that people begin to seek others who share their opinion and discuss how they can prevail for the good of the church. By the time the conflict reaches stage three, people have chosen sides, and each side is committed to winning at all costs. At this stage, the conflict has intensified so much that the pastor cannot lead the church out of the conflict without outside assistance. Failing to resolve the conflict at this point will allow it to escalate to a stage-four conflict in which people are committed not only to winning but to hurting the other side. By this point, the best the mediators can hope to do is to salvage whatever is left and hope the church can rebuild from that.

Repeat Offenders

In unhealthy churches there's often a *pattern* of conflict. These churches continually repeat the same unhealthy practices and wonder why they always experience conflict. Such churches are unable to see a connection between conduct and consequences. A deacon once remarked to a young Christian that he could not understand why their church always seemed to have conflict every time they were on the verge of growing. The young Christian did not respond but thought he was looking at one of the chief reasons. This deacon was one of the controllers in the church who resisted almost every effort to grow. This controlling group kept the church in such a state of conflict that pastors seldom stayed long, especially if they were visionary leaders who wanted to lead the church in new ministries. Unfortunately, that deacon did not see his own responsibility for the church's problems, and nearly three decades later, that same church has still been unable to achieve its potential for ministry.

Pastoral candidates should always inquire as to the tenure of previous pastors and be very wary of a church whose pastors have seldom stayed more than a couple of years. Such churches may well be prone to conflict and resistant to any change that might be suggested. Every church has conflicts, but the conflicts in these churches are usually intense and often dirty and mean-spirited.

Summary

Anytime a group of people are closely connected to one another, there will be conflict. Healthy churches are able to normalize conflict and address it in positive ways. While there are many causes of conflict, the way to resolve conflict is with love and truth. In some churches, controllers create conflict because they want to control the decisions made in the church. Such persons must be confronted and challenged. Their power to control the actions and decisions of the church must be taken from them if the church wishes to achieve its God-given purpose for being.

Healthy churches are able to see conflict as a means by which change can occur in the church. Often it's not a battle between good and evil—it's a difference of opinion about the best choices that can be made. In such cases, conflict allows for growth to occur as people pray and interact with one another to discuss the options available to them. When people are willing to engage in conflict with integrity, good things can result.

8
Spiritual Leadership

If a church is to be healthy and vital, it needs to be led
by a pastor and leadership team who are themselves
pursuing health in their personal lives and
in their shared leadership capacity.[1]

—Stephen A. Macchia

Leaders can operate out of many different strengths. Some are great visionaries. Others are better communicators. Some excel in planning and implementation. The best leaders know they don't have to excel in every aspect of their role in order to succeed. They can bring other people with strengths they don't possess onto the team to help them be more successful. However, the one quality every leader must have to be successful is *character*. A leader who lacks character may enjoy short-term success, but eventually that lack of character will destroy his or her credibility and further opportunities to lead.

In the 1980s the Protestant community saw some of its high-profile leaders fall because of moral failures. Although some of them continue in ministry today, their influence is insignificant to what it was prior to their failures becoming public knowledge. Currently the Roman Catholic Church is struggling with the same issues. Unfortunately, these same failures are found in churches all across North America. While they don't always make the headlines, their effect on the Church is just as serious.

When church leaders fall, a common scenario is often played out. Some people will support the leader regardless of what he or she has done. Others in the church will demand the removal of the leader from further responsibilities in the church. A division occurs that may never be healed. If persons in the church have made the allegations of misconduct, those persons are often seen as the enemy, especially by the leader's supporters. They often find little support for their actions and may even receive threats. New members and seekers may be shocked that such things occur in a church and leave, perhaps never to return. Even when the matter is finally resolved, the church may have problems for many years with issues of trust. During those years little significant ministry takes place.

These problems can be avoided if churches remember that the most important quality of a leader is character. Regardless of how talented or popular a person may be, if he or she lacks character and integrity, he or she has no business being a leader in the church.

This is true for both pastoral and lay leaders. First Tim. 3 gives the spiritual qualifications for pastors and deacons. It's interesting that there are few differences between the two lists of qualifications. Both were expected to be spiritually mature people. We need to ensure that such people are in leadership positions in our churches.

A Spiritual Leader's Agenda

Spiritual leadership is about more than just moral and ethical issues—it's about leading people in accordance with God's agenda for their lives. According to Henry and Richard Blackaby,

> Too often, people assume that along with the role of leader comes the responsibility of determining what should be done. They develop aggressive goals. They dream grandiose dreams. They cast grand visions. Then they pray and ask God to join them in their agenda and to bless their efforts. That's not what spiritual leaders do. Spiritual leaders seek God's will, whether it is for their church or for their corporation, and then they marshal their people to pursue God's plan. The key to spiritual leadership, then, is for spiritual leaders to understand God's will for them and for their organizations.[2]

God's will for a person or a church begins with His desire that we be in a continual state of growth. God is always more interested in our *becoming* than He is in our *doing*. Our ministry will grow out of our personal development into mature Christian disciples. Spiritually immature people can't lead others in spiritual growth.

> Leaders cannot take their people into a relationship with Christ that goes any deeper than they have gone themselves. Followers may grow deeper spiritually in spite of their spiritually immature leaders, but they will not grow deeper because of such people. Thus, spiritual leaders must continually be growing themselves

74

if they are to lead their people into a mature, intimate relationship with Christ.[3]

As an area minister, I work with many churches as they search for new pastors. Our denomination has a profile system that allows them to be able to compare pastoral candidates. The profile includes a place to list any continuing study opportunities the candidate has taken advantage of. I'm always concerned when this section is blank. I encourage the churches to ask about this when they interview their candidates. A pastor who's not continually growing and taking advantage of learning opportunities is one who's unlikely to help others in the church to grow.

I'm just as concerned when I see churches select laypeople for leadership positions who exhibit little or no growth in their lives. These may be moral people with great personal integrity, but if they're not growing as disciples, they can't provide the church with spiritual leadership. They neither understand God's will for their lives nor for the church. God's agenda for the church will be replaced by their own agendas. Such leadership will only cause the church to continue its wandering and miss whatever opportunities for ministry it might have enjoyed. The church will never be healthy until it's led by spiritually mature leaders.

Qualifications for Church Leadership

What should a church look for in its leaders? I suggest that it begin by comparing potential leaders with 1 Tim. 3. Supplementing that scripture, Gene Getz lists 13 qualities of a spiritually mature leader that should prove helpful to churches. He writes that leaders must

1. Live exemplary lives that will be obvious to all people.
2. Be morally pure individuals.
3. Walk by faith and reflect biblical love in their relationships.
4. Be wise and discerning.
5. Live life in a way that makes the gospel appealing to those outside the church.
6. Be generous toward others.
7. Be able to communicate with gentleness and grace.
8. Not be bound to sinful habits.
9. Be able to control anger.
10. Be persons of conviction and willing to take a stand for those beliefs in a manner that also reflects love and grace toward others.
11. Not attempt to control others.

12. Faithfully support the church financially.
13. Maintain good relationships with members of their familes.[4]

Leaders should measure up to very high standards, and those standards should have been observed for some time before installing them into their positions. First Tim. 3:3 says that a pastor should not be a novice, and verse 10 says that persons seeking to serve as deacons should first be tested. It should be obvious to all that the persons placed into positions of church leadership must be spiritually mature people who have the gifts and calling to serve in those positions.

Challenge for the Small Church

What does the small church do when it needs five leaders, and only two people in the church appear to meet the qualifications? Minister with two, and help others in the church grow and mature as believers so that one day they might be qualified. Churches are better off without a pastor or a specific number of lay leaders than to have the wrong people in those positions, especially if those persons are not spiritually mature.

Some small churches struggle with finding sufficient numbers of spiritually qualified leaders simply because of their size. The temptation is to fill the slots with the best possible candidates even if they're not spiritually mature people. This is always a mistake that will end with serious problems in the church. A church can't expect to flaunt the clear teachings found in 1 Tim. and elsewhere and expect God's blessing on the church. In my 25 years of ministry I've never seen a strong, healthy church led by spiritually immature individuals. I *have* seen many small churches deal with conflict after conflict because of the poor leadership they have in place.

Handling Spiritually Immature Leaders

There are really only four ways to handle spiritually immature leaders in the church.
1. Confront them.
2. Live with them.
3. Help them grow spiritually.
4. Work around them.

Confrontation is the most direct way of dealing with such leaders, but I suggest that before you confront them, do a thorough reading of the previous chapter on conflict as well as other books that specifically address conflict management and resolution. In a small church it's likely that these persons have been in leadership for many years, and they'll not appreciate being challenged. A new pastor might well find his tenure severely shortened by such confrontation. At times such confrontation may be unavoidable, but it needs to be approached carefully and prayerfully.

Living with such leadership really isn't a good option either. Chances are that the church has enjoyed little successful ministry for years because of spiritually immature leadership. If poor leadership is creating an unhealthy church, then changes need to be made in the leadership if the church wishes to be healthy.

Some people have never developed spiritually because no one has helped them do so. I discovered as a pastor that I was often better at challenging people to do better than I was at helping them do better. Many laypeople want to grow and develop as Christians, but they need someone to help them understand how to do so. Spiritually immature leaders may be doing the best they can, and if someone will help them do better, they will. Investing in people who want to grow will provide a church with many good returns.

Unfortunately, not all spiritually immature leaders want to grow. They may be the matriarchs or patriarchs of the church who lead because of their power and influence. No one has dared challenge them in the past, and they're now entrenched in their positions. It will not be easy, but the only way to help such a church is to raise new leaders who will be ready to step in when the weak leaders are no longer able to continue in their positions. In the meantime, these newly developed leaders can enable you to work around the positional leaders to accomplish some needed ministry.

Developing Spiritual Leaders

The key is to identify people with leadership potential who have a desire to grow as disciples. Once you identify these people, you need to begin pouring yourself into their lives. You may actively mentor some of them. Identify their strengths, and begin to develop those strengths. You may have special studies specifically designed for them. Help them find conferences and workshops that will help in their development. In short, invest in these people, because they'll become the leaders your church will need.

Be prepared for criticism. Others in the church will complain that you spend too much time with these people. They'll criticize you for neglecting them and their families. A common belief in the small church is that the pastor should spend equal time with everybody. It may be common, but it's wrong and unbiblical.

Jesus modeled an important principle for us. Although He had many disciples follow Him during various stages of His ministry, He concentrated most of His efforts on only 12. From that 12, He had an inner core of 3—Peter, James, and John. While small-church pastors must spend time with everyone in the church, we must concentrate the bulk of our time on that handful who shows the greatest potential to become the leaders of our churches. These are the people who will multiply the ministry of our churches and impact the greatest number of lives.[5]

This takes time and much patience. While you develop these leaders, you'll see many other things in the church that need change. Resist the urge to confront those changes until you get spiritually mature people in positions of leadership. "Do not downplay the importance of developing spiritual giants before trying to transform a congregation. The most important issue in transforming a congregation is the spiritual dimension of the leadership, no matter how much the leaders know about change principles."[6]

I believe any pastor who wants to lead a healthy church must teach sound leadership principles to the current and future lay leaders. Regardless of the church's size, it takes more than one person to have an effective ministry. As a minister and a businessman, I read a lot of secular books on leadership and believe that many of the principles in those books are transferable to church leadership. However, unless a church leader is solidly grounded in the teachings of Scripture and is living out those teachings in his or her life, that person cannot provide spiritual leadership to the church. According to Irvin A. Buesenitz, "Competent leadership is anchored securely to strong biblical convictions and is an absolutely essential quality for effectiveness in ministry."[7]

Final Concerns About Spiritual Leadership

These concerns will not be pleasant to read. Many small churches are at a crossroads. There are some exciting opportunities for ministry today. Whether a church can take advantage of those opportunities depends largely upon its leadership. My fear is that the leadership that exists in many of those churches will prevent them from being used by God in a great way. I see too many pastors who should have retired or gone into secular work years ago. It's obvious from their preaching and their ministry that they long ago lost whatever passion for ministry they had. It's equally obvious that they stopped growing years ago. They lead from a model they learned in seminary, and many of these models simply no longer work.

I also see too many laypeople who lead their churches much the way they conduct their businesses. Pastors are fired with no more compassion than would be seen in a corporate takeover. Decisions are made without congregational input or even knowledge in some cases. These decisions are often made with a "bottom-line" mentality. People who ask questions or express concerns about the way the church is operating risk being verbally or emotionally abused. What ministry does exist is limited to the people within the church.

Of course, I'm not describing the leadership that exists in all small churches. Many small churches with excellent leadership are being used by God to serve their communities. I hope I'm not even describing the majority of small churches. But I *am* describing too many of our small churches that continue to drift around like ships without rudders because of poor leadership.

Before going on to the next chapter, spend some time thinking about the quality of leadership that exists in your church. Is your church being led by people who continue to grow and develop as disciples of the Lord Jesus Christ? Are these spiritual people with high moral values and principles? Do they appear to have a clear vision of what God wants to do in and through your church, and are they pursuing that vision?

It's equally important that you consider your own spiritual development. What has been your spiritual development since you became a Christian? How is your life changing? Do you have a plan to continue to grow and develop? As you continue to become a more spiritually mature person, you will be better able to provide spiritual leadership to your church. Only God knows how that could impact your congregation.

Summary

The most important quality of pastoral or lay leadership in a church is character. It's not enough to ask someone to serve in a leadership role because of his or her education, status, talents, or how long he or she has been a member of the church. Character is more than moral or ethical behavior, although it certainly includes these qualities. It also has to do with whether a person is seeking to live his or her life in accordance with God's will. Spiritual leaders are persons who are growing in their faith. Only these growing individuals should be asked to serve in leadership positions in the church.

Small churches will sometimes have trouble finding enough spiritually qualified persons to serve in various leadership positions, but they must resist the urge to simply fill those positions with the best persons they have. It's far better to let a position remain unfilled than to fill it with someone who's not spiritually qualified to be a leader.

One of the great needs in many churches is the development of spiritual leaders. This will require much time and intentionality on the part of the pastor, but it will be time well spent. At the same time, the pastor must ensure that he or she is modeling spiritual growth in his or her life.

9

A Sense of Community

God made us to be in relationships—with himself and with other people. Highly effective churches have tapped into this inclination by intentionally addressing every person's need to belong to something special. A church that fosters true community is indeed something special.[1]

—George Barna

I was raised in a time when most homes had big front porches that invited friends and neighbors to stop by and visit. People didn't need appointments to visit someone. If they drove by and saw the car outside or the front door open, they would stop and visit for a while.

Things are different today. Our homes are built with no front porches or very small ones. However, many of us do have a big back deck where we can relax behind privacy fences and screen our telephone calls. Nobody can tell if we're home, because our cars are hidden inside the garage, and our front doors are securely locked and the shades drawn. Casual visits are out—appointments are in.

We've paid a high price for our desire for privacy. North Americans are among the loneliest people in the world. Other factors that lead to our loneliness include

- A decrease in marriages
- An increase in divorces
- An increase in the number of single-parent homes
- Fewer children living at home
- An increase of people living alone[2]

Although a few people may enjoy the life of a hermit, most people prefer to be in relationship with other people. We were created to live in community. Loneliness can lead to physical illnesses, depression, and even suicide. On the other hand, healthy relationships with other people can bring much joy and a sense of fulfillment to a person's life.

People have two basic needs today that the church can address: spirituality and community. People need to connect both with God and with one another. Richard Southern and Robert Norton explain that "communities in the past—families, as well as social, religious, and civic groups—were an anchor for people, something that made them feel rooted. But those anchors are no longer holding fast. Families, social and religious institutions, and civic groups are quite different today from what they once were."[3]

People Desire Community

The key theological word of the 21st century is relationship. . . . The challenge of the church in the 21st century is to make itself less of an institution and more of a community; less a place that asks, "What can you do for us?" and more of a place that asks, "What can we do for you?"; less a place focused on better facilities and more a place focused on faith upgrades; less led by people prone to call a meeting than by people prone to start a conversation.[4]

Churches that can provide relationships and a sense of community will find a ready audience. George Barna encourages such churches with these words:

Our research throughout the past decade has shown that this emphasis upon relationships has become increasingly important in attracting the unchurched to attend a church. . . . the Church is unique in that it is intended to be a community—not just an aggregation of unrelated people simultaneously seeking their own benefit, but a group of individuals with a common purpose and a set of explicit relational parameters where true relationships are meant to flourish.[5]

Small Churches Are Relational

We've already discussed how relationships are so important in the small church. This would seem to give the smaller churches an advantage in being able to offer community to people who are desperately seeking it. Unfortunately, this is not necessarily the case.

Most small churches insist they are friendly churches that love everybody. However, if you ask people who visit these churches, a different story is sometimes told. They may have found the church cool and unfriendly. The church members probably did not mean to be unfriendly; it's just that their social needs were already being met by their church community, and they failed to offer that same community to their guests.[6]

I see this too often as I travel to different churches nearly every week. One Sunday I visited one of the small churches in my area. I had not served in my present position very long, and many people still did not know who I was. Since this was my first visit to this congregation, I decided to see for myself how they welcome guests. No one met me as I entered the church, so I picked up the bulletin from a table in the entrance and sat down near the back of the sanctuary. There were very few people in the sanctuary, and the few who were there were in active conversations with one another. I sat in the pew for a few minutes and noticed out of the corner of my eye three people staring at me. I could hear one of them ask in a whisper if the others knew who I was. No one did, and no one made any attempt to speak to me prior to the start of the service.

This congregation probably believes their church is a friendly, warm church. They are partially correct. They are very friendly to their church family, but outsiders will find it difficult to experience that warmth. Unfortunately, this problem exists in too many churches. When a friend of mine visited a small church one Sunday, he was asked to move twice before the service started because he was sitting in someone's pew.

This problem may continue to exist even after a person becomes a member of the church. "Up to one-third of all current members in a congregation at a given time say they do not feel they are truly part of the community of faith,"[7] according to Southern and Norton. This can happen in the small church because people can still be regarded as newcomers even after they have attended there for a number of years. This is especially true if the church has been led for a number of years by one or two families. Unless the small church provides opportunities for all people to experience true community within the church, it will be unattractive to new people and will experience certain decline.

Larry Crabb tells us,

> The future of the church depends on whether it develops true community. We can get by for a while on size, skilled communication, and programs to meet every need, but unless we sense that we belong to one another, with masks off, the vibrant church of today will become the powerless church of tomorrow. Stale, irrelevant, a place of pretense where sufferers suffer alone, where pres-

sure generates conformity rather than the Spirit creating life—that's where the church is headed unless it focuses on community.[8]

How to Create Community

Several years ago a new ministry came into our community and began holding Bible studies. People were asking about this new group, so I decided to visit their study one night. I sat in the city parking lot across from their meeting place for several minutes hoping to see someone walk into the building. No one did. I walked to the entrance and opened the door. In front of me was a flight of stairs illuminated by a single hanging light bulb. I walked up the wooden stairs and heard the sounds of a guitar coming from behind a closed door. For several minutes I listened outside the door until I heard the entrance door open behind me and footsteps began coming up the stairs. I still remember taking a deep breath and opening the door into their meeting area.

I'm glad I attended their Bible study for two reasons. One, I found out that the group was a cult that was beginning to spread out from a neighboring community. I was able to warn people about their false teachings. Fortunately, they did not find an audience in our community.

The second reason I was glad I went was because it gave me a better understanding of how difficult it is for someone to visit a church for the first time. I was confronted with two closed doors before I had any idea of what was going on inside that church. If I, as a pastor, found that troubling, how much more troubling is it for people who don't have a church background? The leader and his wife spoke to me, but they were the only ones who did. When the service ended, they invited me back but never made any attempt to find out how to contact me.

Building healthy relationships begins when a person first steps onto the property. As mentioned before, trained greeters should welcome every person who visits the church. Pick greeters who have gifts of hospitality and helps, who are outgoing and are genuinely glad to meet someone new. Some churches find it helpful to station greeters outside so people can be welcomed in the parking lot.

Guests should be introduced to as many people in the congregation as possible. It's very helpful to introduce them to people who are similar to them in age. If they're not attending with a member of the church, someone from the church should sit with them.

At one time it was common in small churches to ask visitors to stand and introduce themselves. This is still done in many churches, but it's a practice that makes first-time guests very uncomfortable, as it would most people. While they appreciate friendly attention from individuals, most first-time guests would prefer not being asked to make public statements to the congregation.

After the service it's important that the church have a good follow-up strategy. While many people would expect the pastor to call on them after they've visited, it makes a greater impact for someone else from the church to contact them as well. The person who sat beside them during the service is a good candidate for this. This is a good time to find out if the person has any questions about the church, and it provides an opportunity for the church to find out if there are any special ways they can assist their recent guests.

When our daughter and her family moved to another city, they began looking for a church. After visiting several churches, they found one they really enjoyed. That afternoon a couple of women from the church stopped by their house with some jellies and freshly baked bread. Their visit lasted only a few minutes, but it made an impact on the family. They soon began attending that church because they were able to develop a relationship with several of the members.

All this sounds like church growth strategy, but it's really more than that. This is a relationship-building strategy. A healthy small church intentionally looks for opportunities to demonstrate that they care for people. Treating people with respect, honoring them as individuals, and sincerely caring about their needs are necessary ingredients for developing a healthy relationship with them.

Don't underestimate the difficulty your people may have in welcoming these new people to your church. Although most small congregations say they want to see new people come into their fellowship, many of them fail to understand the dynamics these people bring to their churches. These will not just be new members of the church—they'll be new *family* members. Ron Crandall states it well:

> Welcoming new people is not easy, and it uses up psychological energy, even for those who love company.
>
> One reason for the difficulty is that church visitors and new members in small churches are not merely "company" or "guests," as it is sometimes put in megachurches. Rather, they are potential or actual new family members waiting to be adopted. Making company feel welcome is a much different and less threatening task than adopting new family members.[9]

Maintaining Healthy Relationships

Developing healthy relationships can be difficult, but it may be even more difficult to maintain those relationships. Churches are made up of many different people with varying expectations, personalities, and life experiences. Eventually these differences will clash. How well we handle those clashes will determine how successful we'll be in maintaining our relationships.

I'm greatly concerned about the lack of grace I see in many of our churches today. I've heard Christians say terrible things to one another because of a difference of opinion about some minor issue. Pastors are attacked, and sometimes fired, for the most minor failure to meet someone's expectations.

The pastor of one small church found himself in trouble with a few members of the congregation over a minor issue. For nearly a year he had to explain his actions. He admitted he used poor judgment, apologized, and promised the church leadership and his accusers that he would not make the same mistake again. While this satisfied most of the congregation, a few would not let go of the matter. While he was away for a week's trip, the lay leadership met and decided to demand his resignation. He returned from his trip and was told that his resignation was expected by the next day. If he resigned, the church would provide him with three months severance pay. He did resign, and then the leadership informed him they had decided to reduce his severance pay to two months. There's little grace in unhealthy churches.

This pastor had only been there for two years. The congregation was excited when they called him as pastor, and he felt the same excitement. Good things were happening until he failed to meet the expectations of a handful of people. The good things were quickly forgotten, the minor mistakes were magnified—and another pastor found himself out of a job.

Gal. 5:15 warns us, "If you bite and devour one another, beware lest you be consumed by one another!" This church prides itself on its friendliness and sense of community, but their fellow churches don't see them that way. I suspect that people living in their community don't either. This church wonders why they can't grow, but the reason is likely to be that they've acted this way in the past toward other pastors and probably other people as well. Francis Schaffer said it well: "Our relationship with each other is the criterion the world uses to judge whether our message is truthful—Christian community is the final apologetic."[10]

Community in Action

I recently was told a story of a church who modeled community after the death of their pastor. This occurred during the Great Depression, and the church owed the pastor some salary when he passed away. The lay leaders determined that they would see that his widow received the money the church owed her husband. Since the church did not have the money, the leaders decided they would personally pay it, but they didn't have the money either. They began to dig rock out of a local creek, crush it into smaller stones, and sell it to the county for roadwork. In doing so, they paid every dime owed their former pastor. This is a story of community in action. It reminds me of another story found in Acts 2:44-47:

> Now all who believed were together, and had all things in common, and sold their possessions and goods, and divided them among all, as anyone had need. So continuing daily with one accord in the temple, and breaking bread from house to house, they ate their food with gladness and simplicity of heart, praising God and having favor with all the people. And the Lord added to the church daily those who were being saved.

The world has always looked for a place where true community is practiced, and today is no exception. When our churches exhibit true community, when people know they'll be welcomed, loved, and respected, they'll begin to listen to the Good News we have to tell them.

Summary

Loneliness is a major problem for many people. Many desperately want to experience relationships with others and hope for some community in which those relationships can occur. Small churches have the opportunity to be that community because of their normal tendency to be very relational organizations, but such a community does not happen automatically. We have to ensure that our churches are safe places for our members and guests. We have to demonstrate by our actions that we're genuinely interested in other people, not just in what we hope they'll contribute to our churches. We must be willing to extend grace toward others just as we've been the recipients of God's grace. Offering such a community will draw the hurting and lonely to our churches and enable us to share with them the good news of Jesus Christ.

10

Financial Health

Most leaders assume that everybody who comes to church knows God's mind on financial matters. But the truth is that many people today are absolutely clueless regarding the basic principles of Christian financial management. Leaders and teachers need to educate their congregations before they can expect them to honor God with their money and eventually get excited about resourcing the church.[1]

—Bill Hybels

Mention the word "stewardship" in many small churches, and the stress level immediately begins to soar. Even though the leader may clearly teach that stewardship involves the wise use of our time and talents as well as our treasures, people immediately associate stewardship primarily with money. We don't like to talk about money in the church. It just isn't a proper topic for a family to publicly discuss.

But we *do* discuss it in church. Often we discuss the lack of money whenever someone proposes a new ministry or when it's time to prepare next year's budget. It's certainly a topic of discussion when the church considers the pastor's salary and benefit package.

As an area minister, I often work with churches seeking new pastoral leadership. Nearly every time, I hear some version of the following statement: "We would like to be able to offer a larger salary, but we're just a small church, and we don't have much money." My response is always the same: "You don't have a money problem. Your church has either a vision problem or a stewardship problem. Your church either lacks vision, or you have people who are robbing God every week with their tithes and offerings." By this time I have their attention, so I explain to them what I mean.

People Give to a Vision

People are not interested in giving money to pay the utilities and the pastor's salary. They'll provide the money needed to do that in order to keep the church open, but their giving will be minimal. Church leaders who are effective in raising money do so by speaking about the issues and ministries that motivate their people.

George Barna's research among people who donate money to churches and charities reveals six primary motivations that lead people to give their money. He states that at least three of these motivations must be met before people will give their money.[2]

1. A desire to make a lasting difference in the world.
2. The expectation of receiving personal benefit from the work done by the group.
3. The existence of a personal relationship with people of influence in the organization.
4. A personal relationship with others who support the organization.
5. The desire to meet an urgent need being addressed by the organization.
6. The appeal of the organization's efficiency in its operations.[3]

People get excited when a church leader has a vision that goes beyond merely maintaining the present order of things. Unfortunately, many small churches exist without a vision of what God wants them to do or be. The people drift from Sunday to Sunday without any real purpose or direction. They dutifully attend services each Sunday, sit in the same pew, and give the same amount to the offering that they've given for years. At the business session each month the financial report is read, and if the budget has broken even for the month, everyone goes home content. But there's never any money for ministry beyond the maintenance items necessary to keep the church open, which means there's little likelihood for any growth.

As I explained in chapter 4, a healthy small church is led by a vision. The congregation has a vision that goes beyond a maintenance mentality. They're serving the Lord with a purpose that energizes them, and they support that purpose with their financial giving. Allow me to share examples of two churches and how they responded to a vision.

Three men from a small church went on a mission project to Mexico. One of the men had been to this mission station previously and was familiar with the people and the work they were doing. Shortly after returning home, he received a letter from the mission station asking for assistance. Another team of workers was scheduled to arrive soon to put a new roof on the school. The anticipated funding for the materials for the roof had not come through. Without those materials there would be nothing for these workers to do. The materials would cost $13,000, and the director of the mission project asked if their church could help raise this money.

The church had a business meeting scheduled shortly after the man received this letter, and there he shared the needs of the mission station. The three men had previously shared with the congregation their experiences of working there, so the church was familiar with the project. After discussion, the church voted to donate the entire $13,000 to the mission station.

This offering represented several years' worth of normal mission giving for this church. Although its denomination made it easy for the church to give to the various denominational mission offerings, it never made a compelling reason for them to give. Its denomination provided envelopes, a program, flyers, and posters, but it never touched the hearts of the people with a compelling vision. The people gave to the denomination's mission offerings, but they could never see what happened with their money. Their money disappeared in a fund somewhere marked for "missions," but they never knew exactly how their money made a difference in the world. Their mission support in the past had been solid, but they had never made a gift like the one they did to this school in Mexico.

This time they could see the difference they were making. They could see a roof over a school built to teach children. I can count five of Barna's six motivations listed above at work in this situation. The people were given a vision that was bigger than they were—and they responded.

In chapter 4 I mentioned how the church I pastored in Indiana went about the construction of its new fellowship building. Using this as my second example, here is a little more about what happened. As you may recall, before I resigned from my pastorate at this church, we voted to construct this new facility. After we eventually had an architect draw plans and a sketch of the building, we were ready to move forward. I scheduled a commitment Sunday to see just how committed we really were to this building. Fifty people attended the service. We received our usual collection and then conducted the special offering. People could either give cash gifts or make pledges for up to two years. That morning our people gave $54,000 to this new building.

There was great excitement in the church when the total was read. People had caught the vision of the building and the new ministries it could support. We immediately scheduled a ground-breaking ceremony and began the project.

When I was asked about financing the building, I replied that I believed we could complete it without financing. Please understand that I did not rule out financing, but I knew we had enough money to start, and I just believed God would provide the resources. I wanted to give God room to work rather than simply running to a banker and asking for a loan.

I resigned from the church shortly after the subfloor was put down. When I announced my resignation, some people voiced their concerns about the future of the building project. I tried to assure them that they would build it just fine without my leadership and that I still believed it would be built without having to borrow funds.

Two years later the new building was completed. It's a beautiful facility that adds so much to the church. The total cost was just under $200,000, and it was built completely debt-free. This church of 50 people paid for this building as it was being constructed because they had a vision of something much bigger than anything else they had ever done. Not only did God provide them with the vision, but He also provided them the resources needed to see that vision fulfilled.

Sometimes when I tell this story, people ask about the makeup of the congregation. This is a typical small rural church. No doctors, lawyers, or other professional people attend there. Many in the congregation are retired, and the others work in sales, offices, or in other blue-collar jobs. However, they're not typical in their willingness to move forward in an exciting way to fulfill God's vision for their church.

Incidentally, during this building project the church continued to support its denomination's mission offerings at an amazing rate. A few years earlier the church voted to give 15 percent of its offerings to the primary mission offering of its denomination. They did not waver from that commitment during the building project and gave approximately $12,000 each year to that offering. Not only did they have a vision for a new building, but they also maintained their vision for missions.

People Need Stewardship Training

I recently met with a committee from a small church who brought up their financial difficulties. After listening to them talk about their money problems, I asked how long it had been since the church had any training in stewardship. The chair asked, "Stewardship—what's that?" I told her that her response indicated just how important it was that their church have stewardship training. I began to briefly discuss stewardship, and she got very agitated when I mentioned tithing. She said, "I'm giving as much as I can to the church, and I don't want anyone telling me that's not good enough." Although I did not agree with their former pastor's decision not to teach stewardship in this church, I certainly understood from her reaction why he was reluctant to do so.

The Bible clearly teaches that the tithe belongs to God (Mal. 3:8-9). The word tithe means "a tenth." However, the average Evangelical Christian is giving only 3.5 percent of his or her money to the church.[4] Clearly, many Christians are in direct disobedience to God in the area of their finances.

If every church member gave his or her tithe to God, the Church would have more than enough money to do the work God has given it to do. Because so many people don't tithe, many churches have a much reduced ministry. Other churches rely on fund-raising methods to finance part of their ministry. They depend on yard sales, soup suppers, booths at the county fair, and other schemes to raise money. How is God honored by someone buying an old hat or a bowl of oyster soup to finance His work? On the other hand, bringing our tithes and offerings and giving them to God is an act of worship in which He is honored. God's way is always best, and His way of financing the work of the church is through the tithes and offerings of His people. There's a great need today for our congregations to be taught these truths.

Who is the best person to teach stewardship in the small church? It's probably not the pastor. This doesn't mean that pastors should not preach on stewardship. In fact, the opposite is true—they must preach about stewardship if they're going to be faithful to preach the whole counsel of God. But when they're the primary persons teaching stewardship in the church, motivation questions will abound. People will wonder if the pastor is preaching about money because it's the right thing to do or because he or she wants to increase the giving level of the church in order to get a pay raise.[5]

Others should take the lead in stewardship instruction in the church. Sometimes denominational leaders can come into a church and help develop stewardship programs. Many stewardship programs are available through nondenominational organizations that can be used in the church. Don't make the mistake of thinking these programs are just for larger churches. Many of them can be tailored to any size of church, and some are developed specifically for small churches. Respected laypeople can be effective leaders of these programs.

Stewardship training should be an annual event. References can be made to stewardship principles throughout the year in sermons and Bible studies, but the church should have an annual emphasis on stewardship. We live in a very materialistic society that calls us to a consumer mentality. We need to be reminded on a regular basis what the Bible says about the proper place material things should have in our lives. We need to be reminded that all we have has come from God. It's His, and we're merely stewards of it. We need to be reminded that God is glorified through our giving. In short, our churches need an annual stewardship emphasis because we can easily forget what the Bible teaches about this important subject.

Modeling Financial Responsibility

One of the primary ways to teach stewardship is through your own example. Do you tithe to your church? Some pastors believe their ministry is their tithe, but I would challenge them to support that scripturally. Does the church know you tithe? This can be sensitive, but there are some ways to let the church know you not only believe in biblical stewardship but also practice it.

When I was a pastor, I always dropped our tithe check into the offering plate as the ushers came forward. Rather than have my wife put our check in the plate from the pew, I wanted the church to see me put in our check. This was done very quietly, but anyone looking toward the pulpit area could immediately see that we were giving our financial contribution.

During one sermon on stewardship, I shared with our congregation about how I struggled with tithing in my early walk with God. Although I believed in tithing, our financial situation when we were saved made it very difficult to do so. We gradually increased the amount we were giving, but we did not tithe during the first years of our walk with God. I also shared about how God honored the desire we had to tithe, and within a few short years our finances were in order—and we've faithfully tithed ever since. Some of our church leadership later stated how powerful that testimony was to them and the church.

It's very difficult to be so open about finances, but the pastor must take the lead and share his or her own commitment to financial responsibility. Bob Russell, pastor of Southeast Christian Church in Louisville, Kentucky, was challenged to announce to the congregation what he would give to their building campaign. Southeast Christian Church is one of the exciting megachurches in North America today. Over 14,000 people attend services there every weekend. In 1992 the church voted to relocate and began a $26 million campaign to purchase property and build a new facility. The firm they hired to assist in the fund-raising effort asked the pastor to give a personal testimony about what he planned to give. Although he was very reluctant to do so, the firm insisted that it was important the congregation know of his personal commitment to the project.

The pastor wrestled with how to discreetly announce what he was giving. He was preaching four messages on stewardship, and in one of those sermons he told the congregation, "In the last campaign, I joined with three other leaders in borrowing ten thousand dollars each to give to the church. This campaign is five times larger, so I've decided to give five times as much."[6]

The congregation knew the leadership was not asking them to do anything they were not personally doing themselves. The church raised more than the campaign goal and built a beautiful facility that offers exciting ministries to a large region.

Teaching About the Other 90 Percent

Stewardship is not just about tithing and giving to the church but also about how we manage all that God has given us. We live in a very materialistic society in which we're constantly bombarded with offers to buy more and more. Young people go off to college and find their mailboxes filled with credit card offers. "Buy now and pay later" has become the motto for many consumers today. Recent reports on the news have stated that personal debt has increased to dangerous levels, while savings have declined to the lowest levels since the Great Depression.

The Church has a wonderful opportunity to help our society by teaching about financial responsibility. Regardless of size, any church can conduct classes on financial responsibility. Videos and prepared lessons are available from reputable Christian financial organizations that present the material from a biblical perspective. Bankers and financial planners are usually willing to address such classes. Persons who request financial assistance from the church can be encouraged to attend these classes, and some churches require it before assisting the person a second time.

Fair Pastoral Compensation

A financially healthy church will be generous in the salary and benefit package for their pastor. Although some small churches are responsible in this area, others are unwilling to financially compensate their leadership adequately.

I recently conducted a survey of the bivocational ministers in my denomination. Completed surveys were returned from 110 persons, and the salary and benefits many of them receive is very disappointing. The average cash salary for the males responding to the survey is $9,770, while the average cash salary for the female ministers is $8,578. The most common benefit received by these bivocational leaders is mileage reimbursement.

One pastor reported that he receives a cash salary of $3,900 per year with no additional benefits. He has served that church for seven years, and even though the church has seen both spiritual and financial growth during that time, he has never received a salary increase. Another pastor reported serving three small congregations with a total salary from all three churches of $6,120 per year.[7]

Scripture clearly teaches that churches have a responsibility to provide for their pastors. A healthy small church will want to compensate its pastoral leadership in a manner that is fair to both the church and the individual. Many denominations can offer guidelines about fair pastoral compensation and provide churches with figures from churches of similar size that churches can use for comparison purposes.

Summary

A church will never be healthier than its finances. When churches struggle each month to merely pay their utility bills and the pastor's salary, they can't fulfill their ministry to those outside the church. Churches that face constant financial problems usually suffer from a lack of stewardship training or a lack of vision. Many small-church pastors are reluctant to address financial matters from the pulpit or conduct any type of stewardship training in the church. In some cases, they've been ordered not to do so by lay leaders in the congregation. The Bible is not reluctant to talk about money, and neither should the pastor if the church is to be healthy and vital.

Finances usually improve in a church when the congregation clearly understands that their gifts are going for more than maintenance items. People want to financially support ministry, not maintenance. It's amazing how much money can be found in a church when people understand the exciting things that will be done with their money.

Healthy churches ensure that their pastoral leadership is fairly compensated. Scripture is clear that the church has an obligation to provide for its pastor. The excuse about a lack of financial ability is not sufficient reason to expect the pastor and his or her family to suffer financially.

11
Mission-Mindedness

True health does not mean personal or corporate well-being. It means personal or corporate productivity. . . . The mere health of the body of Christ is meaningless unless it blesses all humankind.[1]

—Thomas Bandy

Organizations, people, and churches go through a predictable life cycle, which includes birth, growth, maturity, old age, and death. For a church it's acceptable to use the terms "birth," "growth," "plateau," "decline," and "death." The birth and early years of a church are exciting as a new ministry begins to attract people and the church grows. Unfortunately, that excitement will wear off as the church reaches maturity and reaches a plateau. No organization can remain on a plateau for long, and a long, gradual decline soon begins. Some believe that churches will begin to plateau and start their decline after about 20 years.[2]

The most frightening aspect of this is that this process is irreversible. Individuals cannot reverse their life cycles, and neither can churches. What a church *can* do is to start a *new* life cycle before the church declines so far that it cannot be saved. Ideally, while the church is still in the growth stage, it would start a second life cycle. However, the reality is that few churches are willing to start something new when they're so successful at what they're doing. Most churches will wait until they've plateaued or are declining before trying to move in a new direction. Aubrey Malphurs explains why it's dangerous to wait so long to start new ministries:

> When a church waits until it is dying to make changes, it finds itself in a reactive, not a proactive, mode. It may be too late to start a new sigmoid curve. The church may have used up much of its resources in trying to keep the sinking ship afloat. Few people are

willing to invest in a ship that is listing badly, and many head for the lifeboats. Those who decide to stay with the ship find themselves constantly wrestling with discouragement.[3]

A new life cycle will begin when the church becomes more mission-minded than survival-minded. Once a church reaches maturity, it often becomes focused on itself, but such focus will ultimately lead to its death. God did not call our churches into existence in order that they might merely survive. He called them to impact the communities where they're located for the kingdom of God.

Bill Easum sends a strong warning to churches content to merely survive: "I really doubt if God cares much whether our meager institutions survive, but I do know that God cares about Christians being light, leaven, and salt to the world."[4]

Church Growth-Minded or Mission-Minded?

Quite often churches ask me to help them find ways to grow. When I ask why they're interested in growth, they usually respond that they realize they're dying and that if they don't do something, the church will not be able to support itself. The fear of dying is not an adequate reason for a church to want to grow and will usually mean the church will *not* grow.

I was recently contacted by the leaders of a church who indicated that they needed assistance in growing. Their congregation was growing older and smaller, and they needed to find ways to reach new people. I suggested they consider a new church transformation process we were beginning to implement, and they invited me to share it with the congregation.

I preached in the church that morning and talked about the need to transform our churches to enable us to more effectively reach our communities for Christ. I shared how our new process could assist their church in that transformation, but I also told them it would probably lead to some conflict and the possibility that some people might leave the church because they would not want to experience the transformation.

After the service, I met with the congregation to answer any questions they might have. One of the first comments referred to the possible conflict I had mentioned in the sermon. The individual said that when I made that statement, she looked around the room and couldn't see anybody she was willing to see leave the church. Nearly everyone in the room agreed, and I haven't heard anything else from that church about wanting to grow. The sad thing is that these are good people who know their church is dying, but they're more committed to maintaining what they have than they are to being on mission with God.

Mission-Mindedness Requires Us to Look Beyond Ourselves

To be on mission with God means we have to be committed to doing whatever He calls us to do. Sometimes that will require us to do some things that are uncomfortable or far beyond anything we've ever considered doing before. But as Leonard Sweet explains, "The church does not define its mission. God does. It is God's mission in the world that concocts the church, not the other way around."[5]

This is challenging for most churches, but it's especially so for the smaller church. We're so caught up in our traditional ways of doing ministry that we don't think we can do it any other way. We automatically scratch any idea that doesn't fit with how we've done things in the past. Besides, we argue, we're too small to be doing new things. Our limited resources must be protected in order to ensure our survival. Such thinking robs us of the opportunity to be used by God in some exciting new ways.

A new pastor began serving a small church, and the church soon began to grow. His ministry generated excitement in the church, and the people soon began to search for new ways to do ministry. They significantly increased their mission giving, but they were not content with merely providing money for missionaries. They wanted to do mission work themselves and indicated a desire to minister in a needy area a few states away. When they told me of their desire to make contact with someone in that area, I remembered another church that already has a very effective ministry there. I helped the two pastors connect with each other, and the smaller church has now made its first mission trip into the area.

The people of this small church are not doing this because they want their church to grow. Their efforts will not necessarily cause any of the people they're serving in this area to join their church. They feel called by God to do this work, and they're committed to being on mission for Him. I predict this church will be so transformed by this ministry that they'll attract other people to Christ and to their church. Their growth will be a by-product of their willingness to be on mission with God. For this old, small rural church, this ministry will be a new life cycle leading to new excitement and new life.

Two Hard Questions

In his powerful book about the Church, Paul Brand describes how cancer is caused by healthy, functioning cells that disregard the rest of the body and attack normal cells. He then compares these cancer cells with the Church and writes, "My only message is the caution of a doctor: remember, the body will have health only if each cell regards the needs of the whole body."[6]

A healthy church is one that cares more about serving others than in its own survival. It's committed to being on mission with God in the world and making an impact on the community that God has given it. In order to do that, churches must answer two difficult questions. The answers to these questions will decide whether the church is mission-minded or survival-minded.

The first question is "Who are we here for?" This question must be asked on a regular basis and will have a major impact on the planning of the church. Most churches today answer that by deciding that they're here for themselves. Although they would not be likely to verbalize such an answer, one can see it in their budget, their planning, their staffing, their programs, their worship services, and the decisions they make in their business sessions.

Such churches are deeply committed to ensuring that their members receive the entitlements they deserve because of their church membership. Such entitlements include free weddings for their children, their choice of music and worship styles, programs designed to meet their needs, assurance that their pews will always be available for them every Sunday, and quick visits from the pastor every time they sneeze or stub their toes. Other privileges of membership include never having to worry about stewardship sermons, never being asked to do anything that might be uncomfortable, knowing everybody who enters the church, and always discerning the will of God by a 51 percent majority vote.

A church that decides it exists to be on mission with God will also reflect that answer in its budget, its planning, its staffing, its programs, its worship services, and the decisions made in its business sessions. Money will be budgeted for outreach and mission efforts and not merely maintenance items. Rather than having an evangelism committee or mission committee, the church will have teams of people actually involved in doing ministry outside the walls of the church. Pastoral leadership will be selected who can train and equip the church members to do ministry (Eph. 4:16). Such leadership will not be expected to do the entire ministry in the church but to equip others to do that ministry. Worship services will reflect music and styles of worship that will appeal to people the church is committed to reaching for Christ and not reflect some nostalgic desire to return to the Church of the 1950s. When proposals are made in business sessions, decisions about them will be based on how well they can help the church fulfill its God-given mission and not on how they might affect the church matriarch and her family.

A second question that's even more challenging to ask and answer is this: "Is what we're doing here really worth the life of our Lord?" Not only should every church ask itself this question each week, but every committee and board within the church should also ask itself this same question at the start of every meeting.[7]

Small churches do have limited resources. Fewer people means less money is available for ministry and a limited number of people are available for the church's various activities. Many times people find themselves on four or five committees and involved in teaching Sunday School and singing in the church choir. They're worn out by their over-commitment to the church, and still they feel guilty because they sense they should be doing even more.

A church that's on mission with God will examine every activity that occurs in the church and evaluate whether or not it's still needed today. Just because something was needed in the past does not mean it must be continued today. Too many good Christian people are overworked in the church because they serve on committees and boards that are no longer productive. Is the work of this committee or board worth the life of Jesus Christ? Is this why He died? If not, then it should be eliminated and the people freed up to fulfill the new mission God has given the church.

More than a Mission Statement

A few years ago churches became convinced they needed to become more like corporate America and develop mission statements. While a mission statement can have value, it can also detract from being mission-*minded*.

Churches sometimes spend months developing mission statements. Often they compare the statements other churches have prepared after they've spent months studying the mission statements of still other churches. Although they're usually worded slightly differently, most of these statements sound very much alike. One must wonder if the statement is really worth all the time and effort that went into it. This is especially true if the mission statement ends up like so many: They are developed, approved by the congregation, and promptly placed in a folder somewhere never again to see the light of day unless someone asks if the church has a mission statement.

It seems to me that Jesus gave the Church a mission statement. We call it the Great Commission and the Great Commandment. In the Great Commission Jesus said,

> All authority has been given to Me in heaven and on earth. Go therefore and make disciples of all the nations, baptizing them in the name of the Father and of the Son and of the Holy Spirit, teaching them to observe all things that I have commanded you; and lo, I am with you always, even to the end of the age (*Matt. 28:18-20*).

The apostle John records the Great Commandment, in which Jesus says,

> A new commandment I give to you, that you love one another; as I have loved you, that you also love one another. By this all will know that you are My disciples, if you have love for one another (*John 13:34-35*).

Rather than spending time studying the mission statements of other churches, we should spend time studying these two statements of mission and then prayerfully determine how they should direct the ministry of our congregation. Essential to this determination is understanding the community where we minister and the needs that exist in that community. When we ask the question "Who are we here for?" the correct answer is that we're here for that community. When we ask the second question, "Is what we're doing here really worth the life of our Lord?" the correct answer is yes if we're meeting the needs that exist in our community.

Supportive of Other Missions

Our churches are only a small part of the Body of Christ. Around the world missionaries are working hard to advance the kingdom of God in some very difficult situations, and our churches have a responsibility to support that work. Some small churches refuse to financially support mission work, using their size and limited resources as an excuse. I believe very strongly that God honors churches that honor mission work, and every church should be committed to supporting missions around the world with their prayers and financial support.

For many years our church gave 10 percent of its offering to our denomination's mission fund. Our rationale was that if we taught tithing, then we should model tithing in our own giving as a church body. A few years before leaving the church, I asked the congregation to increase that amount to 15 percent of our offering. I proposed we do it in increments of 1 percent a year so it would not seem like such a large amount at one time. Although there were some concerns, the decision was made to accept my proposal. That church continues to give far more to missions than other churches of comparable size, but as they have increased their giving to missions, they've also found their total offerings have increased, and they have far more money to use in local ministry than they ever had before. God continues to honor that church's commitment to His work around the world.

Healthy small churches will be on mission with God at home and around the world. They understand that their reason for existence is not merely to survive but to extend the kingdom of God through their efforts, prayers, and finances. They refuse to focus on their limitations but choose to concentrate on the gifts, resources, and opportunities God has provided them. Such a church is an exciting place in which to worship and serve.

Summary

Churches don't die overnight. In most cases they've been on a plateau for many years until death finally overwhelms them. The way to prevent this is to continually start new life cycles by becoming involved in new ministries to people outside the kingdom of God. This requires the church to be willing to look beyond its own needs and preferences and look at the needs of others. Only then can a church truly be on mission with God. Although many congregations claim to be interested in reaching people outside the church, their budgets and programming indicate that the majority of their ministry is for those who are already part of the church family.

Not only does the church have a responsibility to people in its community, but it also has a responsibility to people around the world. The Great Commission does not call us to be interested only in our Jerusalems but also in the entire world. God has called missionaries to serve Him throughout the world, and He has called each local church to support their efforts. Healthy churches look for ways to better impact their communities and to support God's work around the world.

12

Long Pastoral Tenure

To become an effective pastor in a small congregation takes time. Nearly all the ministers identified as unusually effective either by other pastors of small churches or by lay leaders we surveyed have one characteristic in common: they currently serve, or in the past have served, the same small congregation(s) for many years—often a decade or more. Effective pastors of small churches are willing and able to persist in a ministry.[1]

—Tony Pappas

Anyone who has read my books on bivocational ministry knows how strongly I feel about long-term pastorates in smaller churches. I served my church for 20 years before accepting a ministry position in our region, and it wasn't until the seventh year at that church that many of our members trusted me enough to allow me to provide leadership to the church. Other bivocational pastors with whom I've spoken about this topic share similar stories.

The church in which you serve has been shaped by its past. It's a system that's been impacted by events and persons throughout its history. Only a long-term pastorate allows us the opportunity to understand the church and why it does the things it does. However, such a pastorate does not usually happen by accident. Small churches are often seen as stepping stones to larger, more significant ministries elsewhere. Some pastors never unpack their bags when they move to a new church. Almost from the first day, they begin searching for the next church that will become available. Until this mind-set is changed, our small churches will never develop the kind of ministry that will enable them to effectively reach their communities. These churches will never have the opportunity to become healthy. We need a new mind-set among the leaders of small churches that will see these churches as something precious in God's sight and capable of providing top-quality ministry to their communities. I appreciate Tony Pappas's strong comments on this matter:

> Small churches face a number of challenges as they seek to be faithful in the twenty-first century. They also have a needed message of faithfulness for the days ahead. Will small churches succeed in fulfilling God's will for them? Time will tell, of course, but it seems to me that the greatest single resource to appropriate God's tomorrow is *quality leadership*—leadership that seeks God's heart, leadership that loves the small church, leadership that understands the nature of the small church and can act appropriately within it.

> This type of leadership cares about the small church. It believes that each congregation is a magnificent creation of the almighty God and that each congregation is called to a ministry that it alone can accomplish. It believes that each congregation, no matter how small, is a mission outpost in its time and place. And it believes that each congregation has its own wonder and beauty that, by believing in it, can be released.

> This type of leadership is committed, to God and to these people, for the long run. One of the worst things to befall the small church is revolving-door leadership, especially pastoral. Pastoring in the small church is not a job, a function to be done until the five o'clock whistle blows. It is a relationship, a covenant, a marriage if you will.[2]

Smaller Churches Keep Getting Bigger

We often call churches that average 50 people or fewer on Sunday morning "small churches." These churches have typically been pastored by retired pastors, seminary students, bivocational pastors, or lay leaders. The average tenure in these churches has usually been very short, sometimes measured in months. The revolving-door pastorates meant that such churches were doomed to continue their plateaued or dying existence unless some drastic changes occurred.

Churches that averaged between 60 and 80 people were often caught in the middle. They wanted a fully funded pastor, but their finances usually did not allow it. Even if they were able to call a pastor, he or she usually did not stay very long but soon moved on to a larger church.

Once churches reached an average attendance of 100, they were often able to provide more adequate salaries, perhaps a parsonage, and enough ministries to attract seminary-trained pastors who might stay longer. However, this scenario is quickly changing.

Lyle Schaller suggests that "one possible scenario for 2018 is that most of the 225,000 Protestant churches now averaging under 120 at worship that survive . . . will be served by bivocational ministers and bivocational teams."[3] In many of our denominations, a church of 120 people is still considered a pretty strong church, but it appears that even these churches could soon have trouble attracting pastors who will be committed to serving them for an extended period of time. The reasons for this are many, and we'll briefly mention just some of them.

- *Salary and benefit packages continue to climb, putting a lot of financial pressure on churches.* Many churches are finding it difficult to continue meeting the rising costs of health insurance alone, much less being able to offer their pastors a salary increase. I know some pastors who have not received a salary increase in three years due to the increased costs of their health insurance. Only the larger churches will have the financial ability to provide adequate salary and benefit packages to attract and keep pastors and staff.

- *Studies continue to show that fewer pastors are willing to serve smaller churches.*[4] No doubt part of the reason for this is financial, but other factors are also involved. Many spouses of pastors work in jobs that may prevent the clergyperson from moving to a new location. Seminary-trained clergy may feel their gifts and education will not be adequately used in smaller churches. Fewer ministry resources in the smaller churches also make them less attractive.

- *Seminary-trained pastors often find they were not prepared for ministry in smaller churches.* Seminaries train pastors in theology, church history, biblical languages, administration, and programming. All this training is needed by pastors, but it's not sufficient preparation to serve the small church. Small churches are not driven by programs but by relationships. Most people in smaller churches are more concerned about how well their pastor can relate to them as persons than they are about how skillfully he or she can exegete scripture. Maybe the reason so many seminary graduates drop out of ministry after only a short time is due to their struggle to relate to ministry in smaller churches, which are usually the kind of churches to which they're first assigned. That struggle leads to them questioning their call until they finally drop out of ministry completely.

Bivocational Ministry

As Schaller indicates above, smaller churches will increasingly be served by bivocational ministers in the future. Presently, many of the in-between churches consider calling a bivocational minister as a step backward, but in fact it may be one of the best things they can do to ensure their effective ministry in the future.

Not long ago I conducted a survey of bivocational ministers in the denomination I serve. A total of 110 bivocational ministers from around the United States responded to the questionnaire; the average tenure of these bivocational ministers was 5.9 years. This is higher than the average pastoral tenure of 3.8 years.[5] Based on my experience, this is also much higher than the tenure smaller churches experience when they call student pastors, retired pastors, or poorly paid, fully-funded pastors.

Tenure is important, because the primary hope for plateaued and dying small churches is pastors who will remain there long enough to effect a significant turn-around. George Barna writes that "many pastors experience their most productive years in ministry between their third and fifteenth year of service."[6] The average tenure of pastors who effectively reach unchurched people for Christ is 11.8 years.[7]

Small churches who call bivocational pastors are not settling for a less-effective ministry but may be doing the one thing they can do to ensure a more successful ministry. They're calling a person who may better be able to understand their church, their community, and God's vision for ministering in that environment than the person who merely sees the smaller church as a stepping-stone to a more effective ministry elsewhere.

The Harm of Premature Exits

Although the average tenure of bivocational pastors is higher than that of other pastors, there's a disturbing tendency on the part of some to abandon their church at the first sign of difficulty. Such premature exits do great harm to the small church and help keep the church in its plateaued or declining state.

Leaving a church at the first sign of problems adds to the poor self-esteem many small churches feel. Members of smaller churches often believe they're not worthy of good pastoral leadership. The constant changing of their pastors over the years reinforces that belief. Bivocational ministers have often told me that their church is always expecting them to announce they're leaving for a better church. Only time will convince those churches that the pastor is staying with them for the long haul.

Prematurely leaving the church destroys the hope of those who wanted change. Many small-church members eagerly want to see their churches change and have a more effective impact on their communities. They simply don't know how to lead that change, and their prayer is that their pastor does. However, as we've seen earlier in this book, change will always produce conflict. If the pastor leaves at the first sign of conflict, those hoping for change will begin to question whether change can ever occur in that church. Transformation can never happen in a church that doesn't believe it can happen.

Finally, when the pastor leaves at the first sign of problems, it increases the power of those who resisted the change. Just as there are people in most churches who want to see change, there are also those who oppose it. They'll fight change just as hard as they can, and if they can succeed in forcing the pastor out, their power is increased, making less likely the chance of any future change.

Determination Is Required

Small-church ministry is tough, and it's not for everyone. No one serves a small church for the money or the prestige. There's not likely to be much recognition from the denomination, nor will many small-church leaders be asked to lead conferences and retreats. Resources will always be limited, and the time demands will always be great. The leaders of small churches will often find their ideas unappreciated and seen as a threat to the survival of the church.

There will be much frustration with the small thinking exhibited by many in leadership positions. They'll often feel that they and their families are seen as outsiders in the family church. Fellow pastors will sometimes question their commitment to the ministry and wonder what shortcomings exist in their lives that keep them in small-church ministry.

The challenges to small-church ministry are many, and the rewards are few, but one can enjoy a very successful ministry in the smaller church if he or she will stay long enough to overcome these challenges and see God's vision for the church fulfilled.

Keys to a Long-Term Pastorate

We can see some other important keys to a long-term pastorate besides determination. Perhaps one of the most important is having a good fit between the church and the minister. One of the reasons I enjoyed such a good ministry at my pastorate in Indiana was because the congregation and I connected well with one another. I had lived almost my entire life in the same county as the church. The church was located in a rural area, and my wife and I were raised on farms. Culturally, we were a good fit with the church.

We also enjoyed a good fit theologically and doctrinally. We might not always agree on the best way to minister to the community, but we each knew we were in agreement on the doctrines of our faith. A minister will not likely last long in a church with significant theological and doctrinal differences between the church and the pastor.

It's important that the minister and the church begin a new pastorate with the intention that this will be a long-term relationship. It's unrealistic to expect great things to happen quickly, and yet many ministers and church members get frustrated if they don't see changes occur almost immediately. Three small-church pastors contacted me in the past three years wanting to leave their churches after serving less than a year. They explained that they were tired of not seeing any results from the work they were doing.

One of the lessons this chapter teaches is that it will take time to enjoy an effective ministry in a small church. I tell every small-church pastor that anything worthwhile that will happen during his or her ministry in a church will probably take much longer than anticipated. Scripture teaches that the Christian life is an endurance run, not a sprint. We're encouraged to "run with endurance the race that is set before us" (Heb. 12:1). The ministry must be lived in the same way, and we will be much more effective if we take a long-term view of what we are doing.

Having said this, I also admit that it's not easy for most of us called into ministry. I often joke that I think microwaves take too long, but I'm only partially joking. Many of us are type A personalities, and patience is not easy for us. We do want to see immediate results, because we believe that what we do is important. We won't be very successful in ministry, and the churches we serve won't be very healthy, if we don't learn to commit ourselves to a long-term view.

I recently read a book to help me reinforce this in my own life. Stewart Brand has written a clever book designed to help people begin to think long-term. The book is titled *The Clock of the Long Now* and describes a clock that "ticks once a year, bongs once a century, and the cuckoo comes out every millennium."[8] Such a clock would give each of us a different view of time, help us be more responsible, and reward patience. It would also make us more effective in our ministries.

Another key to a long-term pastorate is having a fresh vision for the church. Since we've already addressed the importance of vision in previous chapters, we won't spend much time on it now except to point out that without a vision there's not much reason to remain at a church. A common excuse people use when they begin seeking another church is that they feel they've taken their current church as far as they can. This can certainly be a valid reason for leaving, but it can also be another way of saying that they've lost God's vision for the church. They can't take the church any farther because they don't know where the church is to go.

A vision helps keep goals before the church and gives it a direction in which to move. It keeps ministry fresh and exciting. When you reach one target, you find that God has set up another one a little farther out, and you begin working to achieve that one only to repeat the process again and again. Before long you look back and realize you've been at the church much longer than you thought, but the time went by so fast because you were on God's mission.

Ministers and churches must experience steady educational and spiritual growth if they hope to enjoy a long-term relationship with one another. Some ministers reach a certain level of education and expertise and stop growing. They don't attend training opportunities or read up on new ways of doing ministry. They also stop growing spiritually. Their sermons, prayers, and testimonies all sound just as they did 20 years ago. After two or three years they use up all the sermons in their sermon barrel, so they decide it's time to move on.

To preach and lead the same people for an extended period of time requires more discipline and hard work than some ministers are willing to give. Most ministers I know are willing to do the hard work that enables them to be faithful to the calling God has placed on their lives, but the ministry is also a good place for lazy people to hide. Such people would do the kingdom of God a favor if they found something else to do, because the churches they serve will never be healthy as long as they're there.

We also need to address the church as well. Many churches prefer the ruts they're in and will oppose any changes that might be proposed. They prefer to be where God has been rather than where God is going. Many pastors have been excited about a new ministry possibility only to have it shot down by the same people who complain that the church is dying. Sometimes these pastors' hearts are so wounded that they just stop trying. They correctly understand that if they don't get away from such a church, they'll eventually give up on the ministry. They move on, and the naysayers complain once again about the lack of commitment on the part of today's ministers.

In a healthy church both the minister and the congregation are growing and seeking new ways of understanding God's vision for their church. Determined to be on mission for God, they're committed to learning new skills and taking risks to be faithful to God's calling. In such an environment, a long-term ministry that will produce great results is possible.

Support Is Needed

Small-church pastors need a lot of support if they're going to stay in their churches for an extended period of time. Denominations, judicatory leaders, seminaries, and others who are involved in supporting and developing pastors need to examine how they can better equip small-church pastors with the resources they need. Tony Pappas was a bivocational pastor for many years and now serves as the Executive Minister for the American Baptist Churches of Massachusetts. He offers five suggestions that these organizations should consider:

1. It is vital to identify the persons who will be able to effectively serve small churches.
2. It is important that experienced mentors be assigned to assist these small church leaders as they begin their ministry.
3. Seminaries must begin to teach students the practical skills they will need to effectively serve smaller churches.
4. Ministers who have not had seminary training need a good orientation about small-church ministry.
5. Denominations and judicatories must find ways to develop supportive relationships among small-church clergy.[9]

Such support will enable bivocational and other small-church pastors to be more effective in their ministries and encourage them to remain in their places of ministry. As the pastors of these small churches remain in their churches for longer periods of time, these churches will continue to be healthy and vital congregations.

Summary

It takes a long time for a pastor to earn the trust of a congregation so he or she can actually provide effective leadership. Unfortunately, too many pastors of small churches resign before earning that trust. These revolving-door pastorates are responsible for many small churches being stuck in unhealthy modes. Such churches become unwilling to try new ministries because they've been conditioned to expect pastors to leave about the time they begin something new, leaving the churches to do the cleanup work. In most cases, healthy small churches have been led by the same pastors for a number of years.

There are many reasons why pastors leave smaller churches after only a short time, but all are correctable. Seminaries, denominations, and others must find ways to better equip ministers to serve smaller churches, and resources must be developed to support the smaller churches as they fulfill their God-given ministries.

For many small churches, calling a bivocational minister may be the best solution to their leadership needs. Bivocational ministers tend to stay at their churches longer and may better understand the community and its needs. Also, studies indicate bivocational ministers provide very good leadership to their churches.

13

Involvement in Outreach

A biblical, Christ-centered church should
be involved in growth. Evangelism should be
incorporated in all aspects of the church life.[1]

—David Baldridge

Small churches should find reaching new people for Jesus Christ to be rather easy. The Institute of American Church Growth surveyed 14,000 church members and found that 75 to 90 percent of them came to Christ and became members of their churches because of a personal relationship with a friend or relative.[2] Because relationships are the key ingredient of ministry in small churches, their outreach efforts should be very successful. But if they were successfully reaching new people, they wouldn't be small family churches for very long—so something else must be going on.

Jeff Woods has probably identified the problem:

> The metaphor of family is another commonly used metaphor by congregations. Unfortunately, most congregations have an internal image in mind rather than an external image when thinking of family. While used almost universally by smaller congregations, the family metaphor can limit a congregation desiring to embrace something new by reducing its sense of existence to something private rather than public. The metaphor particularly limits congregations from embracing the new ideals described in this paper because it presents the role of the pastor as one of personal presence and intimacy rather than as one of catalyst for change. While the family metaphor emphasizes relationships, it does not emphasize *new* relationships. It emphasizes space for the existing members rather than space for the newcomer.[3]

Smaller churches talk about wanting to grow and bringing new people into the church, but the reality, as observed earlier, is that most of these churches are quite comfortable and do not want to do anything that will disturb that comfort level. Chapter 9 discussed the sense of community that is often a strength in the small church, but there's also often a fear that if new people are brought into the church, that sense of community will be lost.

A small church recently contacted me about their desire to grow. I was asked to meet with a committee that had been formed to explore some ways in which the church might grow. I asked the caller if there were specific things they would like for me to address. He replied that one thing the committee would like to know is how they could change some things in the church that would help reach new people without upsetting any of the current members!

Mission Stations

We saw in chapter 11 that healthy churches are committed to being on mission for God. That mission is clearly spelled out in the Great Commission given to us by Christ. The mission of the Church is not merely to survive or to provide entitlements to the members. The mission of the Church is to reach out to those persons who don't have a personal relationship with God and to lead them into a growing relationship with Him. According to William Easum,

> Nurturing members of the church for the sake of those members alone is not the mission of the church. It does not matter how small or large the congregation is; the mission is still the same. The purpose of the church is to win the world to faith in God through Jesus Christ. The purpose of the pastor is to equip people to build up the Body of Christ. The purpose of the laity is to pass on to others the new life God has given them. The goal is never simply to "run the church," no matter what size the church may be.[4]

One helpful thing that small churches should do is to stop seeing themselves as churches and to begin to see themselves as mission stations. We now live in a postmodern, pre-Christian world that does not know or appreciate our values or beliefs. Despite the numbers of people who consistently tell pollsters that they're Christians, many people, even church people, don't know what that really means. The lives of Christians are shockingly similar to the lives of those who claim no religious faith. Our churches today minister in the midst of a large mission field, and the work of a mission station is much different than the work of a church.

When one goes to the mission field, there are new languages to be learned, new foods to eat, new cultures to understand, and new stories to hear. To effectively enter into and impact the mission field, we must first understand it and then translate the biblical story into a message that can be understood and accepted by the culture we seek to reach.[5]

Churches have their own language, their own culture, and their own stories. Too often we expect the unchurched to enter our world and adapt themselves to our culture if they want to encounter Christ. That may have worked four or five decades ago when there wasn't such a wide difference between the two cultures, but it's not a strategy that will work in the 21st century. We must enter their world and love them as Christ loves them.

Christ's Example

Jesus Christ was born into a very hostile world. His nation was governed by Roman forces that treated the Jews with hostility and brutality. Religious leaders placed undue burdens upon their own people. Rome tolerated all religions as long as they posed no political threat to their power. The leper and the infirm were reduced to begging for their survival and considered outcasts and sinners by the people. Racial hatred was strong, especially between the Jews and the Samaritans.

When Christ began His ministry, He did not establish a church and invite people to come and learn a new language, a new way of worship, and a new worldview. He went out into that hostile world, embraced it, and met people where they were in their lives. He rebuked the hypocrite while offering forgiveness to the woman caught in adultery. He touched the leper, the blind, and the other outcasts of society and brought healing to their lives. He allowed others to touch Him and receive the healing their bodies and souls needed. He taught them words of truth that transformed people's lives and even took those teachings to the Samaritans. He wept over the condition of the people and continually offered them a message of hope. He did not spend time attacking the culture but worked to change the culture one person at a time. At the end, He paid the ultimate price by giving His life for the salvation of all who would believe in Him.

I find it fascinating that with all the power that was His as God, He never chose to use that power to change the culture. He simply chose to move within that culture and change people's lives.

The Disciples' Example

The Book of Acts not only teaches us how the Early Church was begun but also gives us a blueprint for how effective ministry will be done in the 21st century. The Early Church grew despite hostility and persecution. The disciples were soon forced to leave Jerusalem due to this persecution. As they traveled about in that hostile world, they shared the message of Jesus Christ, teaching in the synagogues and the marketplace and meeting in homes. At times they had to flee for their lives to escape capture, and sometimes they did not avoid their enemies. More than once they were arrested and ordered to cease speaking about Jesus. But their love for Christ was stronger than their fear of people, and they would not be silenced.

The political leaders resisted them, the religious leaders resisted them, people whose livelihood was threatened by their message resisted them, but they overcame all obstacles and continued to tell everyone about Jesus Christ, and churches were formed throughout the world. In a time of great despair, people found hope in Jesus Christ, and they embraced Him and the salvation that He offered.

We Live in Similar Times

The United States is no longer a nation that embraces Christian values and beliefs. The postmodern mind-set opposes any statements that claim to be absolute truth and embraces all worldviews as equally valid. Despite assurances given by politicians during election time, our government today merely tolerates religion. Ravi Zacharias states it well: "In the Greco-Roman world . . . all religions were considered to be equally true; to the philosophers, they were equally false; and to the magistrates, they were equally useful."[6]

Do you see the similarities to the time in which Jesus and the disciples lived and the time in which our churches minister? This is why it's imperative that we become mission stations, because only that mind-set will enable us to effectively minister to the culture in which we live.

What the World Seeks

According to the Alban Institute, the primary question unchurched people are asking is "How can my life work better?" Is the church helping them answer that question, or is it trying to answer questions people aren't asking?[7] Ron Martoia explains how this is also similar to people of the first century:

Those seeking out Jesus in the Gospels did so with tremendous human need driving their quest. . . . We are simply out of touch

116

with the general population of unchurched if we think people come to our churches for any other reason. I have yet to meet a person from the ranks of the outside observer who decided to attend our church because they had some intractable theological question or wanted a deeper understanding of the biblical material.[8]

The First-Century Model of Evangelism

We see now that we minister in the same type of hostile environment as the first-century Church, and people today are seeking the same answers they sought back then. Our churches need to return to the Book of Acts for a blueprint of how to reach this culture for Jesus Christ. One of the obvious things we find is that a great deal of relational evangelism was occurring. Acts 2 records that the people gathered together on a regular basis, sharing their food and their lives, and the chapter concludes by telling us that God added new souls to the Church each day.

We've now come full circle in this chapter. The model used so successfully in the first century is the model that is most appropriate for the small church today. In healthy small churches people are brought to faith in Christ by being brought into the family of faith. Although it does not reach large numbers of people at one time, it's very effective.[9]

An unhealthy small church will not effectively reach out in this way, because it's more concerned with its level of comfort than with outreach, but a healthy church will be excited about the prospect of seeing new people come to Christ and into the church. A healthy church will look for ways to establish relationships with unchurched people, and they'll seek opportunities to share both their faith and their church with their new friends. Such relationships will become doors through which people can enter into a personal relationship with Jesus Christ.

A priority to reach new people for Christ will be reflected in the church budget and calendar. George Barna found that "among the leading evangelistic churches, we found that it was more common to spend 10 percent to 20 percent of the annual budget for that purpose."[10] In another study it was found that out of 100 churches claiming to be committed to fulfilling the Great Commission, 87 percent of them had all their programs targeted to helping believers grow.[11] Does your church claim to be interested in outreach? If so, does your budget and programming reflect that interest, or do they reflect other priorities?

Outreach Must Be Led by the Pastor

Small churches are unlikely to emphasize outreach unless their pastors motivate them to do so. Many churches are so locked in to a survival mode that they simply can't see the great need that exists beyond their walls. Even churches that do have an interest in reaching out to their unchurched community will often not have the training to do it, and they'll need their pastors to provide that training. A number of evangelistic programs are available that emphasize relational evangelism and would be appropriate for smaller churches.

However, it must be emphasized that evangelism is not the responsibility of the pastor. As has often been said, "Sheep have sheep; shepherds don't have sheep." Evangelistic outreach is the responsibility of every member of the church. Some may respond that they don't have the gift of evangelism so they should not be expected to be involved in that ministry. Actually, I've met very few people who had the specific gift of evangelism, but that's not what we're talking about here. Everyone has relationships with other people, and through those relationships we can share our faith and values and invite persons to our church.

Your church should also resist the temptation to form an evangelism committee. Once that committee is formed, evangelism is seen as the work of that committee and not the responsibility of the entire church. The whole church should form the evangelism team of the church, and the pastor must lead and train that team to effectively share its faith with persons within their circles of friendships. In this manner, the small church will have an effective outreach ministry that will be healthy and lead to healthy growth in the church.

Summary

Regardless of size, every healthy church should be involved in evangelistic outreach. Small churches are sometimes reluctant to do so because they fear the changes that might occur if new people are brought into the church. Another reason they may not be evangelistically minded is that they feel inadequate to evangelize. Most people don't feel gifted in this task, and few have received any training in how to share their faith with another person.

It would be beneficial for most small churches to stop seeing themselves simply as a church and begin seeing themselves as a mission station. We currently live in a postmodern era that more closely resembles first-century Christianity than it does the world of 20 or 30 years ago.

The Church today exists in a foreign culture, and we need to learn the language and customs of this culture if we wish to impact it with the gospel. This is the work of missionaries, and small-church members will better fulfill their calling if they begin to see themselves as such.

Church leaders need to prepare their congregations for this missionary service. They need to teach their church members how postmodern people think and believe and to familiarize them with the needs that exist in their lives. Relational evangelism needs to be emphasized. We must also stress that this work belongs to all of God's people, not just those who may be specially gifted in this area or those who have agreed to serve on an evangelism committee. Only when all of God's people become committed to reaching out to those who don't have a personal relationship with Jesus Christ will we be successful.

14

Pursuit of Excellence in Ministry

People expect excellence from their vehicles,
hotels, telephone service—just about everything.
Therefore, they expect it in the church.[1]

—Leith Anderson

This may be the most controversial chapter in the entire book, because it challenges much of what goes on in many of our smaller churches. The small church is one of the few organizations left today that thinks it can still be all things to all people. Stores, businesses, restaurants, and even magazine publishers recognize that they need to specialize in order to be successful. Starbucks did not become the successful company it is today by selling coffee and fishing bait. They concentrated on delivering a specific product to a specific customer, and they're committed to doing it with excellence. Every day thousands of people reward that excellence by buying a cup of coffee at Starbucks.

Small churches seem to think they can take their limited financial and human resources and provide every type of ministry to everyone in the community. They usually end up exhausting their resources while delivering a rather average ministry to a small number of persons. Please don't misunderstand me. These are not bad churches. In fact, many of them are very good churches who want to effectively serve their communities. Unfortunately, they'll seldom be great, healthy churches having the kind of impact for Jesus Christ that they could have.

Jim Collins wrote one of the best business books I've ever read. In his book *Good to Great* he states,

We don't have great schools, principally because we have good schools. We don't have great government, principally because we have good government. Few people attain great lives, in large part because it is just so easy to settle for a good life. The vast majority of companies never become great, precisely because the vast majority become quite good—and that is their main problem.[2]

When I first read those words, I immediately substituted the word "church" for the other organizations he mentioned. We don't have a lot of great churches because we have many good churches, and we're content with that. Besides, it would take too much effort to make our churches great, and there would be some risk in trying to pursue greatness. We might jeopardize the small successes we're currently enjoying to pursue something that few other churches try to pursue. Furthermore, a small church could never be a great church, could it?

Actually, I believe a small church can be a great church. Greatness and success have nothing to do with size, but they have everything to do with attitudes and commitment. A small church can be a great church, but it will require the church to change some of its thinking and begin to pursue excellence in its ministries.

Too Many Ministries

I recently consulted with a small church that was having a number of problems. Finances were down, people were leaving the church, and the leadership was under attack. During the consultation process one thing that quickly became evident was that people were overwhelmed with responsibilities in the church. Some reported they served on four or five committees plus had other responsibilities. They were worn out and felt they were not giving their best effort to the church because they were spread so thin.

When I looked at the structure of the church and the number of committees it had, it was obvious to me that the church was trying to do too many things with the resources it had available. Even though people worked hard, there was not enough time, finances, or skills in the church to do with excellence many of the things they were doing, and the results they were receiving for their efforts were rather poor.

Included in my report was the recommendation that the church take a serious look at the ministries it offered and find just two or three things that fit in with their vision that they could offer with excellence. The people selected to lead these ministries were to be people who have a passion for those ministries and the spiritual gifts that would allow them to do them with excellence. That recommendation, like most of the report, was promptly ignored, and this church remains stuck in its unhealthy ruts.

Focused Ministry Leads to Excellence

Small churches need to rid themselves of the myth that they can meet the expectations of all the people they would like to serve. Part of the problem is that many feel pressured by the ministries of larger churches in their areas, and they feel that if they can't compete with those churches, they'll continue to get even smaller. However, the smaller churches would be far better if they would limit their ministries to a few things they can do well and leave the other ministries for other churches to do.[3]

In his study of successful churches, Barna found that those who were most effective deliberately limited their ministry, allowing their focus to be shaped by the availability of resources and their ability to achieve excellence in targeted areas. The smaller church is exceptionally positioned to practice this principle.

An awareness that God has not called us to be all things to all people can have a liberating effect on the church's mission. It means that we can stop trying to fill round holes with square pegs. Instead of setting programs in place first and then staffing them with the reluctant, the disinterested, or the ill suited, we can begin by designing programs around people's interests and abilities.[4]

When small churches try to compete with the larger churches, it usually causes their resources to be stretched so thin that the ministries they do offer are of lesser quality than the offering from the larger church. That's why people leave the smaller churches for the larger ones. A far better strategy for the small church would be to target a particular culture the congregation would like to reach and develop ministries that would appeal to that target. These ministries would be done with excellence by people with a passion for that ministry and for the target audience.

This is the same strategy used when small stores try to compete with megastores such as Wal-Mart. Anytime a new Wal-Mart comes into a community, a number of small stores close because they can't compete with Wal-Mart's lower prices. The stores that survive are the ones that identify some things they can do better than Wal-Mart, and they focus on doing those things with excellence. They don't try to appeal to everyone with low prices. A convenience store will have much higher prices than Wal-Mart, but people will pay the higher price for the convenience of not having to walk so far and then stand in a long checkout line. A clothing store may begin to carry different brands or different styles of clothing than offered at Wal-Mart and offer excellent personalized service when a customer enters.

Determine Your Focus

Your focus for ministry should be found in your vision statement. If your church still does not have a vision statement, I would encourage you to go back to chapter 4 and read again the reasons a vision is so important. I'm convinced that a church with a vision will be healthier and will be engaged in exciting, rewarding ministry to its members and to the community.

Please do not confuse a vision statement with a mission statement. A mission statement describes why your church exists. As I stated in an earlier chapter, I believe the Great Commission and the Great Commandment provide the church with its mission statement. I see little value in spending much time in discussing mission statements for churches.

However, a vision statement describes how the church will fulfill its mission. The vision statement describes a picture of what the church will look like when it accomplishes its mission. Mission statements are very general; vision statements are much more specific. I see great value in every church having a clear, precise vision statement of how God intends to use that church. Such a statement will help the church focus on those few things that will fulfill that vision, and it enables it to say no to some otherwise good things that would detract the church from its vision.

The next step is identifying the strengths of the church. What are the things your church already excels at doing? One rural church I know has a long history of supporting 4-H. A 4-H group meets there regularly and is very involved in the county fair. As a result, this church has a number of young people with natural connections to it, and it has always enjoyed a strong youth ministry. This is a strength the church would be wise to identify and seek ways to expand.

Another congregation has spent over two years seeking a new pastor. They rejected one candidate because they did not believe he could build a strong youth group for their church. This is a church that has not had any youth ministry for decades, and the small number of people who attend are elderly. Middle-age would constitute the youth of this church. These people might be able to offer a strong senior citizen's ministry to their community and could possibly grow through such a ministry, but it's very unlikely they'll have a strong youth ministry anytime soon.

The mistake such churches make is to think if they pour enough resources and energy into an area of weakness, they can turn it into a strength. The problem is that small churches don't usually have sufficient resources to pour into areas of weakness, and even if they did energize a weak area of ministry, it would probably never really become a strength. Read these wise words from Ron Martoia:

> To invest our time, money, resources, and energy to get all our weak areas up to a baseline minimum leaves us no room, time, money, or energy to source and develop our strength. The result is quite obvious. Strengthen weaknesses, and you'll be an average generalist. Spend time developing the treasure God has invested in you, and you soar as a crucial and high-impact player in God's economy.[5]

Does this mean that the church described above should not do anything for young people? By no means. They need to provide ministry for young people, but this should not become their focus. No church would want to ignore youth or refuse to offer any ministry for them, but this is not going to be a strength for this congregation in the foreseeable future.

Maximize Your Strengths

Small churches will be healthier when they learn to maximize their strengths and manage around their weaknesses.[6] The members of the church above seeking a youth ministry would do better if they identified who they are—a small, rural church of older people—and seek ways to minister to others in their community who are similar to them. Churches will more easily attract people who are most like them. There would be many senior citizens in that community who would benefit from the ministry that church could provide. This is also a target group that's most often neglected when churches talk about who they want to reach.

During a church growth workshop I attended a few years ago, the leader asked the people present to brainstorm target groups their churches would like to reach. The blackboard was soon full of various groups, but no church identified senior adults as a group they were interested in reaching.

It's important for a church to identify who they are, the gifts that exist in the congregation, and the things that people feel passionate about. Each of these are strengths the church can build upon. These strengths should shape the vision of the church and help determine its ministry. The existing strengths are also the things the church should seek ways to improve. Again, recalling the advice of Ron Martoia, when you improve on something that's already a strength, you make it even stronger, but when you try to improve on a weakness, the best you can hope for is to become average in that area.

We must learn to manage around our weaknesses. I love music, but I'm not musically inclined. As a small-church pastor, I had to lead the congregational singing in our church many times, but this was certainly not a strength of mine. I could manage around this weakness by ensuring that our church always had good music leaders. Occasionally, our music leaders would be absent from the service, and I would need to lead the music. I still could manage around the weakness by stepping back from the microphone after announcing the next song we were singing. At least my musical limitations were not amplified—and we were more likely to have people stay for the rest of the service!

Another area of weakness for me was counseling. As a bivocational pastor, I did not have a lot of time to commit to counseling people with problems. I also did not have a strong education in counseling, so I never felt as though I were equipped to enter into a long-term counseling relationship with people. There would be times when people would want to talk to me about some issues in their lives, and I would make the time to do that. But I had to recognize that this is not a strength of mine, and I could actually do more harm than good if I insisted on counseling people with serious problems in their lives. I had to learn to manage around that weakness by referring people to skilled Christian counselors. If it was obvious to me that this was an issue that would need more than a couple of meetings, I asked the person or persons to contact a Christian counseling service near our community and begin to work with them on the issue. I assured them that I wanted to stay in contact with them as they worked through the issue and would be glad to do periodic progress checks with them as their pastor, but their actual counseling needed to come from someone other than me.

Some might say that I neglected our church members with such a policy, but actually I was helping them far more than if I continued to counsel with them. I managed around a weakness in my ministry by referring them to trained persons who could help them far better than I could, while continuing to have a pastoral role with them. I was then free to concentrate on the areas in which I was more gifted and for which I had a passion.

Excellence Does Not Mean Perfection

This chapter discusses the importance of doing ministry with excellence, and I believe such ministry honors God. However, we should not confuse excellence with perfection. Some people are perfectionists and will not do anything unless they can do it perfectly every time. Pursuing excellence is healthful; being a perfectionist is not. There will be times when our best efforts will fail miserably. I've seen many Christmas programs and Vacation Bible School commencements that, despite many hours of preparation and practice, did not turn out exactly as the adult leaders planned. Children would refuse to say their lines or would keep waving to their parents or start crying when they realized so many people were looking at them. In every case the congregation would laugh, and the program would continue. Such is life in the small church.

Excellence is not about perfection—it's about setting high standards and striving to achieve them. It's identifying those ministries that the church can do well and seeking ways to build upon those ministries. It's about training people how to use their gifts in ways that will maximize their personal ministries and the ministries of the church.

Excellence Begins with the Leadership

James Kouzes and Barry Posner write, "Successful leaders have high expectations, both of themselves and of their constituents. These expectations are powerful because they are the frames into which people fit reality."[7] Leaders set the tone for the level of excellence that will occur in their organizations, and this certainly includes churches. Leaders that are content with the status quo, those that are satisfied with average ministries, will lead churches that offer such ministries. I often refer to such ministers as maintenance ministers. Their goal is to reduce the amount of conflict in the church as much as possible and hope to survive until retirement. Leading the church in exciting ministries that will expand the kingdom of God is not even a consideration for such ministers. Actually, such people should not even be called leaders, because they're not—they're maintainers.

Leaders are never content with the status quo but are always seeking a fresh vision from God. They're risk-takers and are committed to excellence in all they do. Such ministry leaders encourage the church to consider new ways of thinking and new ways of doing ministry. They model excellence in their own lives and challenge church members to pursue excellence in their lives as well. They often share with the church their confidence in the congregation's ability to do far more than the congregation often believes it can do. I often told the folks in our church that I believed in them more than many of them believed in themselves. I knew the levels to which they could soar if they would just start believing they could, and it was my joy as their pastor to see many of them achieve much more than they thought possible.

If you're a church leader, I encourage you to set the bar high and challenge others to reach it. When you do reach those goals, reset them even higher. Never be satisfied with the status quo, but always seek a fresh vision from God for your ministry.

Col. 3:17 says, "Whatever you do in word or deed, do all in the name of the Lord Jesus, giving thanks to God the Father through Him." I believe this is a challenge to excellence in all we do, because the things the Body of Christ does and says here on earth reflect Christ. All we do should glorify and honor Him. He deserves our best efforts. A healthy small church will rise to this challenge and seek to do all it does with excellence in order to honor our Lord.

Summary

Small churches must overcome the desire to be all things to all people. It's much more healthful for a church to identify its strengths and focus those strengths on a few ministries they can do with excellence. Excellence is not the same thing as perfection. The church that waits to do things perfectly will do very little. Like so many things in the small church, excellence depends on leaders who are willing to set the bar high and then challenge the church to reach it.

15

Lay Ministry Involvement

One of the most impressive—and important—elements of leadership in the highly effective churches is that most of the leadership comes from the laity.[1]

—George Barna

Every healthy small church I have seen has had strong lay leadership who were involved in ministry within the church and the community. These men and women understood that God had called them to minister using their spiritual gifts and their passions, and they responded to that call. Unfortunately, many other small churches expect their pastors to do all the ministry of the church as well as everything else that needs done.

A few years after I graduated from Boyce Bible School (now Boyce College), in Louisville, Kentucky, I led a revival for one of my classmates. Another classmate, whom I had not seen since graduation, led the worship service each evening. He told me that after graduation he had accepted a church out of state that expected him to do everything. If the grass needed mowing, he mowed it. If the church building needed painting, he painted it. If people in the church needed visiting, he visited them. Following the service one Sunday he was stopped by a woman who wanted to know if he was aware that the light was out in the women's restroom. He replied that he did not know that and asked why she was telling him about it instead of one of the trustees. She replied, "So you can change it. That's what we pay you for!" He resigned a few weeks later.

Every Member Is a Minister

Eph. 4:11-13 reads,

He Himself gave some to be apostles, some prophets, some evangelists, and some pastors and teachers, for the equipping of

128

the saints for the work of ministry, for the edifying of the body of Christ, till we all come to the unity of the faith and of the knowledge of the Son of God, to a perfect man, to the measure of the stature of the fullness of Christ.

The pastor's role in the church is to train and equip the entire congregation for ministry. It's not the pastor's role to do all the work of ministry but to ensure that every church member is equipped to use his or her spiritual gifts in service to God and to the community. I once told the folks at my pastorate in Indiana that one of the happiest days of my life was when I realized they were supposed to pay *me* to get *them* to work! We all laughed, but many in that congregation took their ministry responsibilities seriously and did them wonderfully.

Unfortunately, not all church members understand that God has called them to ministry responsibilities. Elton Trueblood identified the problem:

Perhaps the greatest single weakness of the contemporary Christian Church is that millions of supposed members are not really involved at all, and, what is worse, do not think it strange that they are not. As soon as we realize that Christ's intention is to make His Church a militant company, we understand at once that the conventional arrangement cannot suffice. There is not a real chance of victory in a campaign if 90 per cent of the soldiers are untrained and uninvolved, but that is exactly where we stand now. Most alleged Christians do not now understand that loyalty to Christ means sharing personally in His ministry, going or staying as the situation requires.[2]

Smaller churches can't afford to have people sitting on the sidelines. Limited people resources require that every member of the small church must be engaged in ministry if the church is to have an effective witness in its community. This ministry cannot be limited to sitting on committees and discussing the upcoming Thanksgiving dinner and where the Christmas tree will be located this year. The church needs lay ministers using their gifts and talents in ministries they are passionate about so as to make a difference in the lives of other people. The good news is that there are many laypeople in our churches who want to serve God in this manner. The bad news is that many pastors have not done a good job equipping them to do that.

Pastors Must Train

During my Indiana pastorate I often challenged people to become more involved in ministry. Sometimes I had even scolded the congregation for their lack of involvement. One day I realized I had not done a good job of training them to do ministry. I became very convicted about this ministry failure on my part as I realized that many in our church wanted to be more involved but were depending on me to train and equip them.

In the Ephesians passage quoted above, not only are the saints to do the work of ministry, but also the pastor is to equip them to do so. They could not do their job because I had not done my job. I'm not too sure I was much different from many other small-church pastors I know.

Whom do pastors call when a task needs to be done? We usually call the busiest people in the church, because we know they're the most likely to do it. A case could be made that we abuse our best people and allow everyone else to remain uninvolved. It's easier to call upon the ones who have indicated a desire to serve God and the church than it is to develop others who can also serve. Even if we do ask others to become involved in some aspect of ministry, we often do a very poor job of training and supporting them.[3] Then when they fail, we complain about their lack of commitment.

No one likes to fail at anything, especially if they believe that failure could have been prevented. When we ask people to do ministry in a church but don't train and support them, we almost ensure their failure. We also ensure that they'll be very unlikely to accept another ministry assignment. Pastors must find ways to train and equip people in their churches so those people can effectively minister.

Lay Ministry Development

One fall a group of us from our church attended a John Maxwell seminar in Indianapolis. His organization had developed a program that would help train laypeople in leadership and lay ministry. Our group decided to purchase the material and implement it. I began using the material the first Sunday of the next year, and for six months we did nothing in the church except leadership training and lay ministry development. Sunday morning and Sunday nights we went through this material. Although our church did not have regular midweek services, to supplement what we were doing, I showed videos from Maxwell's *The 21 Irrefutable Laws of Leadership* on Wednesday nights, and then we would discuss the content of the videos.

I was not sure how this would impact our attendance, but our people loved this emphasis. Many said the principles they were learning from this study could be used not only in the church but also in their jobs, their families, and other areas of their lives. It made an immediate difference in our church as more people became involved in ministry to others. We helped people identify their spiritual gifts and then encouraged them to minister in the areas of their giftedness. We challenged people to think of ministries that our church did not have but that they felt called to do. We wanted to be a permission-giving church that would encourage people to use their God-given gifts in ministry without having to have approval from a dozen church boards and committees.[4] Our church became healthier as a result of this emphasis.

There are many tools available to help develop lay ministers. A church pastor should examine different ones to see which would be the best fit for his or her congregation. It would also be wise to get the church's permission before starting such a program, because I've encountered some congregations that would not want such training. Unless they're on board at the beginning and sincerely interested in being equipped for more effective ministry, such training would be a waste of time and money. On a personal note, if my church were not interested in such training, and despite my best efforts to lead them to such interest they remained uninterested, I would take that as a sign that I needed to move on. Not every church wants to be healthy, and pastoral ministry is too short to spend on such churches.

Time Limitations for Lay Ministers

Laypeople have limitations of the amount of time they have available to do ministry. We touched on this some in the previous chapter, but this is a good place to address it again. We live in a very busy time with a multitude of things demanding our attention. Laypeople have many responsibilities to juggle, and they have to determine their priorities. A common trend in some areas is for churches to ask for shorter time commitments. For example, some churches are finding it difficult to recruit people to teach a Sunday School class for a year because people are reluctant to commit that far in advance. They ask people to commit for one quarter or ask two people to alternate teaching a class. More and more people are required to work on Sundays, and alternating assignments may allow some people to be involved who could not be otherwise. If small churches are serious about wanting more lay involvement, they must find ways to adapt to the realities of people's schedules. Healthy churches will do that.

The limited amount of time people have for ministry is one reason a small church must look at its structure. As I mentioned in chapter 6, many small congregations are too structured for their size, with an abundance of committees that require too much time from their members. Again, my suggestion to small churches is that they eliminate their committee structure and develop ministry teams that would be built around their vision for ministry. Most committees could be eliminated from small churches without any reduction in ministry, and with fewer committees there would be more time available for ministry. I've seen a few larger churches do this very effectively, and smaller churches could do it as well. It would allow their members to have more time to effectively minister using the gifts God has given them.

An Absence of Lay Ministers

Some small churches simply have few if any people available to do lay ministry or to provide leadership in the church. Many of these churches will probably not survive unless they take some immediate steps to change this situation. One of my responsibilities is to help churches find pastoral leadership, and as I've noted earlier, it's becoming increasingly difficult to find pastors willing to serve smaller churches. My heart breaks for these congregations, because they almost always consist of some very nice Christian people who were never trained to do ministry. As a result, their churches have declined to the point that they may not be able to be turned around. What can such churches do?

My recommendation is for them to prayerfully consider whether God still has a ministry for that church in that community. It's not always wrong for a church to close its doors, especially if the people in the church can't see a further need for its ministry. However, if they can see where the church can provide needed ministry in the area, they then need to follow the suggestions in this book to restore the church to health. They also need to find some other people who can help them.

If a church simply has no members who can step into a lay leadership position, it might be able to borrow some leaders from a sister church for a short time, perhaps one or two years, until people can be reached and trained. Such people could see this as a mission project as they use their gifts to help a neighboring church develop a healthier, more vital ministry. I know of one church that currently has two former members serving as bivocational pastors in small churches in their community. This church has encouraged and supported these two individuals and their churches, and this is a major contribution to the kingdom of God. Both these men were key leaders in their home church, but their gifts are now being used to turn around two small churches. These two churches were struggling but today are healthier and growing with their new leadership.

Healthy small churches take seriously the mandate to equip and mentor the laypeople in the church. Pastors pour their lives into helping others deepen their spiritual walk with God and equipping them to do ministry. This allows all members of the church to use the spiritual gifts God has given them to do significant ministry in the church and community.

Summary

Healthy small churches have laypeople involved in ministry. They help these individuals identify their spiritual gifts and passions and then begin to equip them to do ministry. The pastor will normally be the primary person responsible for providing this training. An abundance of material is available that's specifically developed to assist the pastor in this training.

Not only do laypeople need to be trained and equipped for ministry, but also they must be released to do ministry. This means they need to be free of committee assignments that require much time but produce little ministry. It also means that the church will help its laypeople decide how to best do quality ministry given the many demands that exist on their time. Furthermore, it requires that the church become more "permission giving" and not require that people jump through so many official hoops before being able to minister in the areas of their giftedness and passion.

16

Time for a Checkup

We've examined several items that make up a healthy small church, and it's now time to examine your own church. I suggest you first do it as an individual and then with the leadership of your church. Take your time, because you want to get this right. Regardless of whether one is healthy or not, the last thing anyone wants is a faulty diagnosis. We want the doctor, the technicians, and the labs to do a thorough job and return with an accurate diagnosis of our situation. It's only when we know something's wrong with us that we can do anything to resolve it. The same is true of the church. If there are unhealthy aspects of our church life, we need to know what they are so we can develop some methods of restoring those areas to health.

A checkup always begins with checking the numbers. The doctor wants to know your temperature, your weight, your blood pressure, and a host of other numbers that he or she will get from your blood work and other tests. The doctor will compare those numbers against a set of numbers considered to be the norm and will also compare them against the numbers you had during your previous checkup.

How are your numbers? Is your attendance up or down? Evaluate your worship service, your Sunday School attendance, the number of people actually involved in ministries, the number of new people who have joined your church, and the number who may have left your congregation. Is the church financially healthy? What's the ratio between your offerings and attendance? Has that ratio gone up or down since last year? You may want to identify some other numbers you feel should be tracked.

Not only is the doctor interested in numbers, but he or she is also interested in obtaining some other information. Here are some questions your church should examine.

Theology and Doctrine
- How would you describe the theology and doctrine of your church?
- Is that theology and doctrine presented in a language that can be understood by the unchurched?
- How many adults are involved in Bible study and faith development?

Vision
- What is your church's vision?
- How many people in your congregation can explain that vision to others?
- How much of your church's ministry and budget is dedicated to fulfilling that vision?

Worship
- How would you describe your church's worship service?
- What specific aspects of your worship service help people experience God?
- Are there changes that need to be made in the worship service?

Change
- What was the last major change your church experienced?
- How did the people respond to that change?
- What was the last suggested change that was rejected by the congregation? Why was it rejected?

Conflict
- How does your church handle conflict?
- Has your church ever split over an issue? What was the issue? Could the split have been avoided?
- Does your church have controllers who are keeping the church from moving forward?

Spiritual Leadership
- How would you rate the spiritual maturity of your church leadership?
- Do your leaders exhibit the qualifications Gene Getz described in chapter 8?
- What specific steps is your church taking to develop future spiritual leaders for your congregation?

Community

- How does your church greet its guests?
- Is there a genuine sense of grace in your church shown toward others?

Stewardship

- Track the financial-giving patterns over the past five years. Is the trend up or down? Why?
- How often does your church provide stewardship training?
- Do your church leaders model tithing in their own giving?

Missions

- Is the primary focus of your church inward or outward?
- For whom does your church exist?
- Is what you're doing really worth the life of the Lord Jesus Christ?

Long Pastoral Tenure

- What's the average pastoral tenure in your church?
- What are the pastor and church doing to make a long pastorate possible?

Outreach

- Do you see your congregation as a church or a mission station?
- How is the postmodern era in which we live affecting the ministry of your church?
- Is the pastor committed to outreach? Are the lay leaders committed to outreach?

Excellence

- Review the structural organization of your church.
- What is the primary focus of your congregation?
- Identify the strengths of your church. How can you improve them?

Lay Ministry

- How many people are involved in ministry outside committee or board assignments?
- Do your members know their spiritual gifts?
- What specific things is your leadership doing to equip the lay-people in your church for ministry?

People would prefer that their doctors find nothing wrong when they go in for their checkup. I wish my doctor had not found I had high blood pressure, but I'm thankful it was found before it had done any permanent damage. With the proper medication, a commitment to exercise, and eating a more sensible diet, my blood pressure is under control.

You may not like the results you get when you give your church a health checkup, but if you can find problems before they have done any permanent damage, you'll have the opportunity to make the needed changes to return your church to health. As your church becomes healthier, you may find it will start growing again. It will certainly have a more positive impact on the lives of your congregation and the community it serves.

We're encouraged to have regular checkups to ensure that we remain healthy. It's the same for churches. The leadership should meet periodically for the express purpose of giving the church a good checkup using these questions and others they may find helpful. The church will certainly want to check its health before beginning any significant new endeavor. Such an examination is also good before calling a new pastor or other staff person. It's always easier to maintain health than it is to regain it, and the earlier you detect a potential problem, the easier it is to resolve.

Notes

Chapter 1

1. Thom S. Rainer, *Surprising Insights from the Unchurched* (Grand Rapids: Zondervan Publishing House, 2001), 124.

Chapter 2

1. Rick Warren, *The Purpose-Driven Church* (Grand Rapids: Zondervan Publishing House, 1995), 17.

2. Dale Galloway, ed., *Taking Risks in Ministry* (Kansas City: Beacon Hill Press of Kansas City, 2003), 38.

3. Steven Burt and Hazel Roper, quoted in *Inside the Small Church*, ed. Anthony G. Pappas (Bethesda, Md.: Alban Institute, 2002), 85.

4. George Barna, *Turn-Around Churches* (Ventura, Calif.: Regal Books, 1993), 22-23.

5. Jim Herrington, Mike Bonem, and James H. Furr, *Leading Congregational Change* (San Francisco: Jossey-Bass Publishers, 2000), 111.

6. Marcus Buckingham and Donald O. Clifton, *Now, Discover Your Strengths* (New York: The Free Press, 2001), 26.

7. Thomas G. Bandy, *Kicking Habits,* Upgrade Edition (Nashville: Abingdon Press, 2001), 58.

8. Jim Herrington, R. Robert Creech, and Trisha Taylor, *The Leader's Journey* (San Francisco: Jossey-Bass Publishers, 2003), 50.

9. Galloway, *Taking Risks in Ministry,* 96-97.

Chapter 3

1. Glenn Daman, *Shepherding the Small Church* (Grand Rapids: Kregel Publications, 2002), 66.

2. Ibid., 23.

3. George Barna, *Boiling Point* (Ventura, Calif.: Regal Books, 2001), 186-87.

4. Charles Colson and Ellen Santilli Vaughn, *The Body* (Dallas: Word Publishing, 1992), 33.

5. John MacArthur Jr., *Rediscovering Pastoral Ministry* (Dallas: Word Publishing, 1995), 254.

6. Ibid., 253.

7. Ron Martoia, *Morph!* (Loveland, Colo.: Group Publishing, 2003), 105-6.

8. Rainer, *Surprising Insights from the Unchurched,* 45.

9. Bandy, *Kicking Habits,* 50.

Chapter 4

1. Dan Southerland, *Transitioning* (Grand Rapids: Zondervan Publishing House, 2002), 24.

2. Andy Stanley, *Visioneering* (Sisters, Oreg.: Multnomah Press, 1999), 18.

3. Thomas G. Bandy, *Moving off the Map: A Field Guide to Changing the Congregation* (Nashville: Abingdon Press, 1998), 183.

4. James M. Kouzes and Barry Z. Posner, *The Leadership Challenge*, 3rd ed. (San Francisco: Jossey-Bass, 2002), 124.

5. Lyle E. Schaller, *Innovations in Ministry: Models for the 21st Century* (Nashville: Abingdon Press, 1994), 96.

6. Bill Hybels, *Courageous Leadership* (Grand Rapids: Zondervan Publishing House, 2002), 48.

7. John P. Kotter, *Leading Change* (Boston: Harvard Business School Press, 1996), 69.

8. Daman, *Shepherding the Small Church*, 220.

9. Ron Crandall, *Turnaround Strategies for the Small Church*, ed. Herb Miller (Nashville: Abingdon Press, 1995), 116.

10. Daman, *Shepherding the Small Church*, 232.

11. Donald W. Morgan, *Share the Dream, Build the Team* (Grand Rapids: Baker Books, 2001), 48.

12. Southerland, *Transitioning*, 75.

13. Leith Anderson, *Leadership That Works* (Minneapolis: Bethany House Publishers, 1999), 196.

14. Herrington, Bonem, and Furr, *Leading Congregational Change*, 62.

15. Kouzes and Posner, *The Leadership Challenge*, 141.

16. Daniel Goleman, Richard Boyatzis, and Annie McKee, *Primal Leadership* (Boston: Harvard Business School Press, 2002), 221.

17. Warren, *The Purpose-Driven Church*, 111.

18. Southerland, *Transitioning*, 147.

19. Ibid., 127.

20. Thomas G. Bandy, *Fragile Hope* (Nashville: Abingdon Press, 2002), 29.

Chapter 5

1. Daman, *Shepherding the Small Church*, 97.

2. Stephen A. Macchia, *Becoming a Healthy Church* (Grand Rapids: Baker Books, 1999), 47.

3. Jack Hayford, *Worship His Majesty* (Dallas: Word Publishing, 1987), 53.

4. Eddie Gibbs, *Church Next* (Downers Grove, Ill.: InterVarsity Press, 2000), 186.

5. Leonard Sweet, *Postmodern Pilgrims* (Nashville: Broadman and Holman Publishers, 2000), 43.

6. Donald E. Miller, *Reinventing American Protestantism* (Berkeley, Calif.: University of California Press, 1997), 88.

7. Thomas G. Long, *Beyond the Worship Wars: Building Vital and Faithful Worship* (Bethesda, Md.: The Alban Institute, 2001), 21.

8. Warren, *The Purpose-Driven Church*, 280-81.

9. Gibbs, *Church Next*, 160.

10. William Easum, *Dancing with Dinosaurs: Ministry in a Hostile and Hurting World* (Nashville: Abingdon Press, 1993), 88.

11. Leith Anderson, *A Church for the 21st Century* (Minneapolis: Bethany House Publishers, 1992), 147.

12. Hayford, *Worship His Majesty*, 83.

13. Galloway, *Taking Risks in Ministry*, 75.

Chapter 6

1. Jeff Woods, "New Tasks for the New Congregation: Reflections on Congregational Studies," *Resources for American Christianity*, 2003, accessed November 8, 2004, at <http//resourcingchristianity.org>.

2. Herb Miller, "Meeting Change-Resistance Challenges," *The Parish Paper*, March 2002, 1.

3. Barna, *Turn-Around Churches*, 38.

4. Goleman, Boyatzis, and McKee, *Primal Leadership*, 226.

5. Anthony G. Pappas, ed., *Inside the Small Church* (Bethesda, Md.: Alban Institute, 2002), 59.

6. Kouzes and Posner, *The Leadership Challenge*, 208.

7. John C. Maxwell, *The 21 Irrefutable Laws of Leadership* (Nashville: Thomas Nelson Publishers, 1998), 173.

8. Ronald A. Heifetz and Marty Linsky, *Leadership on the Line* (Boston: Harvard Business School Press, 2002), 11.

9. Woods, "New Tasks for the New Congregation."

10. John C. Maxwell, *Developing the Leader Within You* (Nashville: Thomas Nelson Publishers, 1993), 58.

11. Margaret J. Wheatley, *Leadership and the New Science*, 2nd ed. (San Francisco: Berrett-Koehler Publishers, 1999), 20.

12. From comments by Doug Murren in *Leaders on Leadership*, ed. George Barna (Ventura, Calif.: Regal Books, 1997), 205.

13. Herrington, Bonem, and Furr, *Leading Congregational Change*, 35.

14. Kotter, *Leading Change*, 4.

15. Ibid., 42.

16. Maxwell, *Developing the Leader Within You*, 52.

Chapter 7

1. Peter Stenke, "Outbreak!" *Leadership*, summer 1997, 47.

2. Maxwell, *The 21 Irrefutable Laws of Leadership*, 33-42.

3. Larry L. McSwain and William C. Treadwell Jr., *Conflict Ministry in the Church* (Nashville: Broadman Press, 1981), 60.

4. Bob Russell, *When God Builds a Church* (West Monroe, La.: Howard Publishing Co., 2000), 158.

5. Ibid., 168.

6. McSain and Treadwell, *Conflict Ministry in the Church*, 117-18.

7. Charles H. Cosgrove and Dennis D. Hatfield, *Church Conflict* (Nashville: Abingdon Press, 1994), 42.

8. McSain and Treadwell, *Conflict Ministry in the Church*, 67.

9. Bandy, *Fragile Hope*, 29.

10. Ibid., 46.

11. Keith Huttenlocker, *Conflict and Caring* (Newburgh, Ind.: Trinity Press, 1988), 83-85.

12. Barna, *Leaders on Leadership*, 244.

13. Heifetz and Linsky, *Leadership on the Line*, 101.

14. Huttenlocker, *Conflict and Caring*, 86-87.

15. Bandy, *Fragile Hope*, 126.

16. Ibid., 125.

17. Ibid., 134.
18. Ibid., 129.
19. Huttenlocker, *Conflict and Caring*, 122-23.

Chapter 8

1. Macchia, *Becoming a Healthy Church*, 16.
2. Henry Blackaby and Richard Blackaby, *Spiritual Leadership* (Nashville: Broadman and Holman Publishers, 2001), 23.
3. Ibid., 128.
4. Barna, *Leaders on Leadership*, 84-103.
5. Galloway, *Taking Risks in Ministry*, 94-95.
6. Bill Easum, *Unfreezing Moves: Following Jesus into the Mission Field* (Nashville: Abingdon Press, 2001), 80.
7. MacArthur, *Rediscovering Pastoral Ministry*, 129.

Chapter 9

1. George Barna, *The Habits of Highly Effective Churches* (Ventura, Calif.: Regal Books, 1999), 82.
2. Robert D. Putnam, *Bowling Alone* (New York: Simon and Schuster, 2000), 277-78.
3. Richard Southern and Robert Norton, *Cracking Your Congregation's Code* (San Francisco: Jossey-Bass, 2001), xxiii.
4. Leonard Sweet, *Jesus Drives Me Crazy!* (Grand Rapids: Zondervan Publishing House, 2003), 103-4.
5. Barna, *The Habits of Highly Effective Churches*, 79.
6. Daman, *Shepherding the Small Church*, 45.
7. Southern and Norton, *Cracking Your Congregation's Code*, 84.
8. Cited in Randy Frazee, *The Connecting Church* (Grand Rapids: Zondervan Publishing House, 2001), 13.
9. Crandall, *Turnaround Strategies for the Small Church*, 119.
10. Cited in Frazee, *The Connecting Church*, 85.

Chapter 10

1. Hybels, *Courageous Leadership*, 105.
2. Barna, *The Habits of Highly Effective Churches*, 148.
3. Ibid., 153.
4. Stephen A. Macchia, *Becoming a Healthy Church*, 199.
5. Barna, *The Habits of Highly Effective Churches*, 149.
6. Russell, *When God Builds a Church*, 245.
7. Dennis Bickers, *Survey of American Baptist Church USA Bivocational Ministers*, 2004.

Chapter 11

1. Thomas G. Bandy, *Road Runner* (Nashville: Abingdon Press, 2002), 94.
2. Gary L. McIntosh, "How to Live to Be 100," *The McIntosh Church Growth Network*, September 1997, 1.
3. Aubrey Malphurs, *Advanced Strategic Planning* (Grand Rapids: Baker Books, 1999), 50.
4. Easum, *Unfreezing Moves*, 23.

5. Leonard Sweet, *Carpe Mañana* (Grand Rapids: Zondervan Publishing House, 2001), 27.

6. Paul Brand and Philip Yancey, *Fearfully and Wonderfully Made* (Grand Rapids: Zondervan Publishing House, 1980), 60.

7. Sweet, *Carpe Mañana*, 170.

Chapter 12

1. Pappas, *Inside the Small Church*, 33.

2. Anthony G. Pappas, *Entering the World of the Small Church* (Bethesda, Md.: Alban Institute, 2000), 9.

3. Schaller, *Innovations in Ministry*, 21.

4. See Patricia M. Y. Chang, "Assessing the Clergy Supply in the 21st Century," Pulpit & Pew Research Reports, Duke Divinity School, 2004, accessed November 4, 2004, at <http://www.pulpitandpew.duke.edu/Chang.html>; and Jack Marcum, "Parsing the Pastor 'Shortage,'" Research Services, Presbyterian Church (USA), 2001, accessed August 12, 2004, at <http://www.pcusa.org/research/monday/shortg.htm>.

5. Rainer, *Surprising Insights from the Unchurched*, 146.

6. George Barna, *Today's Pastors* (Ventura, Calif.: Regal Books, 1993), 37.

7. Rainer, *Surprising Insights from the Unchurched*, 146.

8. Stewart Brand, *The Clock of the Long Now* (New York: Basic Books, 1999), 3.

9. Pappas, *Inside the Small Church*, 37-38.

Chapter 13

1. Quoted in Crandall, *Turnaround Strategies for the Small Church*, 91.

2. Daman, *Shepherding the Small Church*, 153.

3. Woods, "New Tasks for the New Congregation."

4. Easum, *Dancing with Dinosaurs*, 1993, 19.

5. Martoia, *Morph!* 137.

6. Ravi Zacharias, *Jesus Among Other Gods: The Absolute Claims of the Christian Message* (Nashville: W Publishing Group, 2000), 142.

7. Martoia, *Morph!* 188.

8. Ibid., 189.

9. Pappas, *Inside the Small Church*, 167.

10. George Barna, *Evangelism That Works* (Ventura, Calif.: Gospel Light, 1995), 97.

11. Cited in Mark Mittelbert, *Building a Contagious Church* (Grand Rapids: Zondervan Publishing House, 2000), 244.

Chapter 14

1. Galloway, *Taking Risks in Ministry*, 54.

2. Jim Collins, *Good to Great* (New York: HarperCollins Publishers, 2001), 1.

3. Daman, *Shepherding the Small Church*, 246.

4. Pappas, *Inside the Small Church*, 133.

5. Martoia, *Morph!* 41.

6. Marcus Buckingham and Donald O. Clifton, *Now, Discover Your Strengths* (New York: The Free Press, 2001), 26.

7. Kouzes and Posner, *The Leadership Challenge*, 321.

Chapter 15

1. Barna, *The Habits of Highly Effective Churches*, 45.
2. Quoted in Daman, *Shepherding the Small Church*, 179.
3. Herrington, Bonem, and Furr, *Leading Congregational Change*, 74.
4. Easum, *Unfreezing Moves*, 47-51.